Elements of Literature®

World Literature

HOLT ASSESSMENT
Writing, Listening, and Speaking
Tests and Answer Key

- **Workshop Tests in Standardized Test Formats**
- **Evaluation Forms**
- **Scales and Rubrics**
- **Holistic Scoring Guides**
- **6 Traits—Plus 1 Analytical Scale**
- **Sample Papers**
- **Portfolio Assessment**

HOLT, RINEHART AND WINSTON

A Harcourt Education Company

Austin · Orlando · Chicago · New York · Toronto · London · San Diego

Table of Contents

Table of Contents *continued*

Workshop Scales and Rubrics

for Student Edition
pp. 88–1125

Analytical scales and
scoring rubrics for

• Writing Workshops

• Listening and Speaking
Workshops

• Media Workshop

Table of Contents *continued*

Table of Contents *continued*

Overview of ELEMENTS OF LITERATURE Assessment Program

Two assessment instruments have been developed for ELEMENTS OF LITERATURE.

(1) Assessment of student mastery of selections and specific literary, reading, and vocabulary skills in the **Student Edition:**

- *Holt Assessment: Literature, Reading, and Vocabulary*

- *Holt Online Assessment*

(2) Assessment of student mastery of workshops and specific writing, listening, and speaking skills in the **Student Edition:**

- *Holt Assessment: Writing, Listening, and Speaking*

- *Holt Online Assessment*

Diagnostic Assessment

Holt Assessment: Literature, Reading, and Vocabulary contains two types of diagnostic tests:

- The Entry-Level Test is a diagnostic tool that helps you determine (1) how well students have mastered essential prerequisite skills needed for the year and (2) to what degree students understand the concepts that will be taught during the current year. This test uses multiple tasks to assess mastery of literary, reading, and vocabulary skills.

- The Collection Diagnostic Tests help you determine the extent of students' prior knowledge of literary, reading, and vocabulary skills taught in each collection. These tests provide vital information that will assist you in helping students master collection skills.

NOTE: You may wish to address the needs of students who are reading below grade level. If so, you can administer the Diagnostic Assessment for Reading Intervention, found in the front of *Holt Reading Solutions.* That assessment is designed to identify a student's reading level and to diagnose the specific reading comprehension skills that need instructional attention.

Holt Online Essay Scoring can be used as a diagnostic tool to evaluate students' writing proficiency:

- For each essay, the online scoring system delivers a holistic score and analytic feedback related to five writing traits. These two scoring methods will enable you to pinpoint the strengths of your students' writing as well as skills that need improvement.

Ongoing, Informal Assessment

The **Student Edition** offers systematic opportunities for ongoing, informal assessment and immediate instructional follow-up. Students' responses to their reading; their writing, listening, and speaking projects; and their work with vocabulary skills all serve as both instructional and ongoing assessment tasks.

Overview of ELEMENTS OF LITERATURE Assessment Program *continued*

- Throughout the **Student Edition,** practice and assessment are immediate and occur at the point where skills are taught.

- In order for assessment to inform instruction on an on-going basis, related material repeats instruction and then offers new opportunities for informal assessment.

- **Skills Reviews** at the end of each collection offer a quick evaluation of how well students have mastered the collection skills.

Progress Assessment

Students' mastery of the content of the **Student Edition** is systematically assessed in three ancillaries:

- *Holt Assessment: Literature, Reading, and Vocabulary* offers a test for every selection. Multiple-choice questions focus on comprehension, the selected skills, and vocabulary development. In addition, students write answers to constructed-response prompts that test their understanding of the skills.

- *Holt Assessment: Writing, Listening, and Speaking* provides both multiple-choice questions for writing and analytical scales and rubrics for writing, listening, and speaking. These instruments assess proficiency in all appropriate writing applications.

- *Holt Online Assessment* offers tests consisting of multiple-choice questions from *Holt Assessment: Literature, Reading, and Vocabulary* and *Holt Assessment: Writing, Listening, and Speaking.* This convenient online format provides tools with which you may generate and print reports to document student progress and class results.

Summative Assessment

Holt Assessment: Literature, Reading, and Vocabulary contains two types of summative tests:

- The Collection Summative Tests, which appear at the end of every collection, ask students to apply their recently acquired skills to a new literary selection. These tests contain both multiple-choice questions and constructed-response prompts.

Overview of ELEMENTS OF LITERATURE
Assessment Program *continued*

- The End-of-Year Test helps you determine how well students have mastered the skills and concepts taught during the year. This test mirrors the Entry-Level Test and uses multiple tasks to assess mastery of literary, reading, and vocabulary skills.

Holt Online Essay Scoring can be used as an end-of-year assessment tool:

- You can use *Holt Online Essay Scoring* to evaluate how well students have mastered the writing skills taught during the year. You will be able to assess student mastery using a holistic score as well as analytic feedback based on five writing traits.

Monitoring Student Progress

Both *Holt Assessment: Literature, Reading, and Vocabulary* and *Holt Assessment: Writing, Listening, and Speaking* include skills profiles that record progress toward the mastery of skills. Students and teachers can use the profiles to monitor student progress.

One-Stop Planner® CD-ROM with ExamView® Test Generator

All of the questions in this booklet are available on the *One-Stop Planner*® **CD-ROM with ExamView® Test Generator.** You can use the ExamView Test Generator to customize any of the tests in this booklet. You can then print a test unique to your classroom situation.

Holt Online Assessment

You can use *Holt Online Assessment* to administer and score the diagnostic and summative tests online. You can then generate and print reports to document student growth and class results. For your students, this online resource provides individual assessment of strengths and weaknesses and immediate feedback.

About This Book

This book, *Holt Assessment: Writing, Listening, and Speaking,* accompanies the ELEMENTS OF LITERATURE program and provides a variety of assessment resources. These include Writing Workshop Tests and Answer Key, Workshop Scales and Rubrics, Scales and Sample Papers, and Portfolio Assessment.

WRITING WORKSHOP TESTS AND ANSWER KEY

Every Writing Workshop in ELEMENTS OF LITERATURE has an accompanying Writing Workshop Test in a standardized test format. The test format not only will allow you to assess student performance but also will familiarize students with standardized tests and give them experience in test taking.

Each Writing Workshop Test provides a passage containing problems or errors in several or all of the following areas: content, organization, style, and conventions. Students demonstrate their understanding of the writing genre and their revising and proofreading skills by responding to multiple-choice items. Students revise elements of the genre, restructure segments of the passage, add or delete statements, refine language, and correct errors in the passage.

Answer Sheets

Answer Sheets immediately follow the tests in this section. The Answer Sheets correspond to the answer options on a particular standardized test. Use the following chart to help you determine which answer sheet to use.

Workshop	Answer Sheet
Writing Workshops for Collections 1–6	Answer Sheet 1
Writing Workshop for Collection 7	Answer Sheet 2

Answer Key

The Answer Key follows the Answer Sheets at the end of this section of the book. In addition to giving the correct answer, the Answer Key tells which Workshop skill is assessed by each item.

About This Book *continued*

WORKSHOP SCALES AND RUBRICS

This section contains analytical scales and scoring rubrics for Writing Workshops and scales for Listening and Speaking Workshops. Both the scales and the rubrics are important teacher evaluation tools. In addition, students can use the scales and rubrics as learning and evaluation guides for their own work.

The **scales** include essential criteria for mastery of skills and ratings of each criterion based on a four-point scale. The **rubrics** are based on the same criteria listed in the scales. The rubrics clearly describe a student's work at each score point level for each specific criterion.

Score Point 0

On occasion, student work may be unscorable and consequently will receive a score point of zero. This may be true of writing, listening and speaking, and media assignments. The following are reasons to give a product a score of zero. The work

- is not relevant to the prompt or assignment
- is only a rewording of the prompt or assignment
- contains an insufficient amount of writing (or other mode) to determine whether it addresses the prompt or assignment
- is a copy of previously published work
- is illegible, incomprehensible, blank, or in a language other than English

About This Book *continued*

SCALES AND SAMPLE PAPERS

This section contains two different kinds of scales for assessing writing: the 6 Traits—Plus 1 Analytical Scale and the individual four-point holistic scales for biographical or autobiographical narratives, exposition, responses to literature, persuasion, and business letters. Accompanying these scales are high-level, mid-level, and low-level examples of student writing. Individual evaluations, based on the analytical and holistic scales, follow each sample student paper. These scales can be used for on-demand writing or class assignments. Although this section is directed to teachers, students may also benefit from access to this section as they write and revise.

PORTFOLIO ASSESSMENT

This section provides an introduction to portfolio work, including suggestions about how to develop and use portfolios and how to conduct conferences with students about their work.

Forms

The introductory article is followed by a set of student forms for assessing and organizing portfolio contents and for setting goals for future work. Also included is a set of forms for communicating with parents or guardians about student work and for generally assessing students' progress.

Forms in this section can be used to record work, to establish baselines and goals, and to think critically about student work in a variety of areas. These areas include writing, listening, and speaking. The goal of these forms is to encourage students to develop criteria for assessing their own work and to identify areas for improvement. Many forms can also be used for assessment of a peer's work and for teacher evaluations.

Writing Workshop Tests and Answer Key

for **COLLECTION 1**   *page 88*

Writing Workshop: Reflective Essay

DIRECTIONS The following draft of a reflective essay is about an experience that significantly affected a student. The essay contains errors in development and organization. Some of the questions refer to underlined words or phrases or to numbered sentences within the text. Read the essay, and answer questions 1 through 10.

A Little Bit of Kindness

Many of us have felt like outsiders at one time or another. I never gave (1) much thought to my treatment of people on the fringes until Kenneth said (2) that I was his best—and only—friend.

When I started tenth grade, I was desperate to belong. I am planning to (3) go to college, and I studied. As a result, some students called me a (4) teacher's pet. I found out what it's like not to belong, but I wasn't exactly (5) on the fringe. (6)

I quickly became one of the best students in the class. Other students (7) soon learned that I could explain some of the difficulties of geometry and (8) biology in plain English. They might still have looked down on me, but if (9) they needed help understanding an assignment, they were more likely to ask for my help than for the teacher's. Several classmates even asked me to (10) explain easy concepts, such as how to find the area of a triangle.

From my first day in the new school, I could see that Kenneth did not (11) belong. His clothes were shabby and <u>did not fit</u>. Later I heard that he (12) (13) bought most of his own clothes at thrift stores and garage sales.

It never occurred to me to refuse to help Kenneth when he asked me to (14) explain his geometry assignments. Other students began teasing me about (15) being Kenneth's private tutor. I was embarrassed to be seen with Kenneth. (16) I did not want anyone to think that we were friends. Then, in front of the (17) (18) whole class, he blurted out, "You're the greatest!"

The next time he asked for my help, I lied, "I'm too busy." I was afraid (19) (20) that other students might think that I was his girlfriend.

GO ON

When I got home, I thought about what had happened. What had I
(21)   (22)
done to bring this embarrassment on myself? Me, me, me, that's what I
(23)
was thinking about. Then a small voice inside asked, "What about
(24)
Kenneth?" I replayed the scene in my head and focused on Kenneth's face.
(25)
I knew one thing: He was lonely. In the beginning, he did need help
(26)   (27)
with his homework. He thought I was his friend, but he must have been
(28)
wrong about that. A decent, compassionate person wouldn't have treated
(29)
him as I did. "I'm like Kenneth in at least one way," I said to myself. "I'm
(30)   (31)
afraid of being cast out to the margins of the school's social life."

When I got to school the next day, I said to Kenneth, "I'm sorry.
(32)
Anytime you want help with your homework, I would be happy to help
(33)
you. I was just embarrassed by what you said." I left it at that.
(34)   (35)
Now I understand the importance of even a little kindness. I have never
(36)   (37)
forgotten what Kenneth taught me. Since then, I have gone out of my way
(38)
to be kind to students who are ostracized by the popular crowd. I do not
(39)
want fear of what others might think to limit my choice of friends.

---

1 Which sentence or sentences provides the BEST attention-grabbing opener?

A   Kindness is very important.

B   It's hard to be an outsider when everyone else seems to fit in.

C   "You're the greatest!" Don't many of us want to hear those words?

D   Lots of students are lonely and feel as if they don't belong.

2 Which background information would BEST be added following sentence 1?

A   Some students will do almost anything to fit in at school.

B   Two years ago my family moved, and I had to make new friends.

C   This essay is about something that happened to me a while back.

D   A few students don't worry about fitting in.

GO ON ➡

3 To hint at the significance of the experience, which sentence should be added to the end of the first paragraph?

A   Even unpopular students worry about their status.

B   I hoped he wasn't in love with me.

C   I wondered if I shouldn't have helped so many students.

D   That experience changed the way I relate to other people.

4 The organization of the essay would BEST be improved by moving paragraph 4 to follow paragraph—

A   2   C   8
B   5   D   10

5 Which sentence should be deleted to remove irrelevant details?

A   7   C   11
B   10   D   15

6 What is the BEST way to revise <u>did not fit</u> in sentence 12 to add descriptive details?

A   old-fashioned

B   didn't look good on him

C   hung loosely on his thin frame

D   nothing most students would wear

7 To BEST show the relationship between events, which clause should be added to the beginning of sentence 14?

A   Since I didn't like misfits,

B   After math class was over,

C   Since I was used to helping others,

D   After I made the honor roll,

8 Which sentence provides the BEST details to follow sentence 14?

A   He began asking me questions about homework even at lunch.

B   I never wanted to be his tutor.

C   Kenneth's grades were improving.

D   Kenneth was good at math.

9 Which sentence should be added following sentence 24 to BEST reveal the writer's thoughts and feelings?

A   The picture seemed out of focus.

B   I was ashamed when I remembered his look of sorrow.

C   Kenneth was probably embarrassed by the way I had acted.

D   I'll always remember the moment when I realized what I had done.

10 Which sentence should be added to BEST reveal an insight about life?

A   You never know what effect you might have on someone's life.

B   I'm sorry that Kenneth moved away the following semester.

C   I know that I want to have a variety of friends, regardless of what the popular crowd thinks.

D   Most important, I've learned that small acts of kindness can have a major effect on someone's life.

Writing Workshop: Problem-Solution Essay

DIRECTIONS Carlos is writing an essay about the problem of many U.S. students not knowing any language other than English. He proposes that students be required to take foreign language courses in high school. His rough draft contains some errors in organization and development. Read the draft, and answer questions 1 through 10.

Other Languages: An Opportunity for More and Better Jobs

If you could, wouldn't you want to increase students' chances of
(1)
getting good jobs? One way to do this is to increase students' fluency in
(2)
a second language. Even relatively low-level jobs now require fluency in
(3)
a second language. Students should learn another language.
(4)

Except for students who are exceptionally well focused on academic
(5)
studies and those who plan their lives several years in advance, most

students will not choose to take a language elective. Without planning
(6)
ahead, these students limit their choice of jobs and the universities or

colleges to which they can apply.

However, it is not just college-bound students who have limited their
(7)
options. Have you checked out the classified ads for jobs lately? Many
(8)   (9)
jobs require fluency in a second language. Even when the second
(10)
language is not required, it is often listed in ads as "desirable," meaning

that job applicants who know a second language are more likely to be

hired for the position.

Some of the best universities require at least two years of a language
(11)
other than English before they will even consider your application.

Many students wait until their senior year in high school to think about
(12)
college. By then, if they have not studied another language, they have
(13)
already lost the chance to enter some of the top universities.

GO ON ➡

    Police officers and firefighters in large cities are often paid more if
(14)
they are fluent in a language spoken by people in the communities they

serve. For example, bilingual police officers with the Houston, Texas,
(15)
police department receive a pay supplement for their language skills.

Bilingual firefighters in Phoenix, Arizona, receive at least one hundred
(16)
dollars extra per month. Some cities and government agencies reimburse
(17)
employees for the tuition to study another language.

    Studying the grammar, sentence structure, and vocabulary of another
(18)
language often helps people better understand English. My father told
(19)
me that he did not understand the subjunctive in English until he

studied French. My uncle Abraham once told me that studying Italian
(20)
increased his English vocabulary considerably because it caused him to

see the relationships between English and Italian words with Latin roots.

    English is spoken by many well-educated people in all countries, so it
(21)
is easy to claim that we need not learn languages other than English.

Still, we ought to make an effort to learn the native languages of other
(22)
people. Being able to speak and understand another language could turn
(23)
each of us into a goodwill ambassador for the United States.

    It is clear that students need to learn another language or two.
(24)
Learning another language will also help Americans better communicate
(25)
with people from other cultures, whether abroad or within the borders of

the United States. Requiring students to complete two years of another
(26)
language before they graduate from high school will help them prepare

for better and more varied jobs.

GO ON

1 What is the BEST way to revise the opening paragraph to capture readers' attention?

  A   Add a list of jobs requiring fluency in a second language.

  B   Add an anecdote about a cousin who found a job as a translator.

  C   Discuss objections to a proposal for requiring language courses in high school.

  D   Mention solutions that have been tried before, and discuss their flaws.

2 Which sentence, if added after sentence 3, would provide the BEST background information?

  A   Learning another language can be useful if you ever travel abroad.

  B   Some people enjoy studying other languages for the intellectual challenge.

  C   The Sunday edition of the local newspaper listed five entry-level jobs that require bilingual skills.

  D   Some universities have an entrance requirement of two years of a language other than English.

3 How should sentence 4 be revised to make the thesis statement clearer?

  A   Students should be required to study other languages for their own good.

  B   Studying other languages can be fun as well as educational.

  C   Some employers want their employees to know other languages even when the job does not seem to require another language.

  D   To improve students' job prospects, at least two years of study of another language should be required for graduation from high school.

4 The organization of the essay would BEST be improved by moving paragraph 3 to follow paragraph—

  A   1

  B   4

  C   5

  D   7

5 Which sentence BEST elaborates on sentence 17?

  A   Some employers who do not pay for such courses let employees have time off to attend classes.

  B   Some employees think they are too busy to take classes while working fulltime.

  C   However, in a tight job market, a job applicant who already knows the language has an advantage.

  D   You might think that it is better to wait until you get a job so that your employer will pay for the courses.

6 Which sentence should be added before sentence 18 to state the reason discussed in that paragraph?

  A   Learning another language can also improve students' English.

  B   Learning another language can help students get better jobs.

  C   Games and crossword puzzles can be used to help learn another language.

  D   Being able to speak another language makes it easier for someone to do business outside the United States.

7 Which sentence should be added after sentence 22 to BEST address the counter-argument addressed in sentence 21?

   A   We should expect people in other countries to speak English.

   B   It isn't all that difficult to learn another language if you work at it.

   C   Most large cities in the United States have people who can help you learn another language.

   D   This simple effort will help us avoid cultural misunderstandings.

8 Which sentence provides the BEST evidence to be added after sentence 23?

   A   Too often, Americans make a bad impression when they visit other countries.

   B   People in other countries often appreciate that a visitor has made the effort to learn their language.

   C   French used to be the second language of most well-educated Europeans.

   D   For many people, writing another language is harder than speaking it.

9 Which sentence should be added after sentence 24 to remind readers why the proposed solution is best?

   A   Students in other countries study different languages, so it can't hurt for U.S. students to learn a language other than English.

   B   Studying another language will help U.S. students read European literature in the original language.

   C   Adding a language requirement is the easiest way to increase students' job opportunities.

   D   If you learn another language, you won't need to read the subtitles of foreign films.

10 What is the BEST call to action to add after sentence 25?

   A   Let us add a language requirement to help our students become better citizens of the world and of our own country.

   B   Let us start planning our overseas trips to give us a goal to work toward.

   C   Students who learn another language may be able to contribute more to their communities.

   D   Learning another language is a good way to increase your vocabulary.

for **COLLECTION 3**   **page 472**

Writing Workshop: Persuasive Essay

DIRECTIONS Elizabeth's teacher has asked the students in her class to write a persuasive essay using cause and effect. This rough draft of Elizabeth's essay contains errors in organization and development. Some questions refer to underlined words or numbered sentences within the passage. Read the draft, and answer questions 1 through 10.

What a Waste!

The windows of our van were open. When we drove around a small (1) (2) hill, the stench of something rotting nearly gagged us. "Man, look at the (3) trash!" my classmate Latisha shouted. I tried not to breathe. Our driver (4) (5) raised the windows. Latisha coughed and sneezed. I said, "This is the city (6) (7) landfill! We must have taken a wrong turn." That was the day I started (8) (9) thinking about garbage. Lots of cities produce too much garbage. While the (10) (11) situation is daunting, we <u>can help solve the problem</u>.

Many people do not realize how much trash we produce each year. (12) Around the world, manufacturing paper products uses at least 35 percent (13) of the wood harvested each year. In the United States, 40 percent of the (14) trash is paper products. That is a lot of trees gone to waste. (15)

In Australia, some elementary schools recycle. If young children (16) (17) overseas are recycling, we high school students can, too.

Dumping refuse in a landfill is not a good strategy. As a city grows, it (18) (19) has to buy more land for landfills. That land might otherwise be used for (20) parks or businesses. Maintaining a landfill requires tax money, too. (21) Employees collect the garbage that ends up in the landfill. Other employees (22) (23) take care of administrative tasks and record keeping. In tight economic (24) times, we have better ways to spend tax dollars.

While students might not cure the problem, we can help. We can run a (25) (26) school paper-recycling program. Administrators will need to set up the (27) program, but students can take care of day-to-day tasks.

GO ON →

>   I propose that we begin recycling paper products. We use a lot of paper.
> (28)   (29)
>
> A pilot program to recycle paper would reduce the amount of trash and
> (30)
>
> encourage businesses to help finance the program. While we should con-
>   (31)
>
> sider how to reduce the amount of paper we use, we need to recycle.
>
> By committing to buy recycled paper products, we can also save money.
> (32)
>
>   Those who think that recycling would cost too much should consider
>   (33)
>
> the costs of failing to recycle. A little money spent upfront can reduce
>   (34)
>
> environmental cleanup costs. Also, some of the major companies will
>   (35)
>
> probably be willing to help us set up the pilot project. When my cousin
>   (36)
>
> Fernando lived in Baytown, Texas, several oil companies paid for a
>
> community recycling center. I think our local businesses are equally
>   (37)
>
> community-minded. I am sure that when people see the benefits of a
>   (38)
>
> recycling program, they will help us set it up.

1 **Which sentence provides the BEST background information?**

- **A** On landfills near oceans, seagulls cause safety problems.
- **B** Landfills are unsightly.
- **C** On average, a landfill reaches its capacity in about seven years.
- **D** People throw away useful items.

2 **What is the BEST way to revise <u>can help solve the problem</u> in sentence 11?**

- **A** should think more about how we use earth's natural resources
- **B** can reduce the amount of trash by recycling paper
- **C** can help solve the problem if we discuss the causes and effects
- **D** should ask teachers and administrators how to protect the environment

3 **The organization of the essay would BEST be improved by moving paragraph 3 to follow paragraph—**

A	1	**C**	6
B	4	**D**	7

4 **Which sentence should be added following sentence 16 to provide supporting evidence?**

- **A** Lewisville, Florida, maintains a Web site with recycling information.
- **B** Some people keep worm farms to recycle their table scraps.
- **C** No one is too young to develop environmental consciousness.
- **D** Even young students are encouraged to recycle the paper they use.

5 Which sentence provides a strong ethical appeal?

A We can't let those little kids do more than we're doing, can we?

B If young children can recycle, we should feel a similar obligation to protect our communities.

C If young children can recycle, it isn't difficult to recycle.

D We can learn from the recycling programs set up for young children.

6 Which sentence provides the BEST elaboration to add after sentence 21?

A Cities must buy equipment to maintain the landfill.

B It is a very dirty job, but someone must do it.

C Why would anyone want that job?

D My uncle runs the landfill.

7 Which sentence should follow sentence 27 to strengthen the logical appeal?

A Teachers and administrators can tell us what we need to do.

B We should think about the problem.

C We can make sure that very few recyclables end up in the garbage.

D Janitors should probably run the program.

8 Which sentence provides the BEST elaboration to follow sentence 32?

A Someone will buy the paper made from our recycled paper.

B Some businesses might not be interested, but others will be happy to have another customer.

C We can ask businesses whether they are interested in helping us set up the program.

D We can buy recycled paper at a discount in exchange for the office paper that we recycle.

9 What is the BEST way to revise sentence 33 to address a counterclaim?

A We should recycle our paper, regardless of the cost of the program.

B We can easily set up a recycling program if we can find businesses willing to pay the expenses.

C Those who think recycling would cost too much should consider the costs of maintaining landfills.

D After a landfill is full, it may pollute surrounding air, water, and land.

10 What is the BEST call to action to add after sentence 38?

A Let us establish a paper-recycling program now, before we need a new landfill.

B That is why I think we should start small, with the recycling of paper.

C We can later expand the program to include other recyclables.

D Then, tourists visiting our city won't run the risk of accidentally touring mountains of trash.

for **COLLECTION 4**   *page 570*

Writing Workshop: Extended Definition

DIRECTIONS Juanita's teacher has asked the class to write an extended definition of a word. The following is a draft of Juanita's extended definition of *courteous*. The draft contains errors in development and organization. Some of the questions refer to underlined passages or numbered sentences within the text. Read the draft, and answer questions <u>1</u> through <u>10</u>.

What Does *Courteous* Really Mean?

(1) The instructors at my martial arts school emphasize the relationship between courtesy, respect, and gratitude. (2) A dictionary might define *courteous* as only "being polite and considerate." (3) According to my karate instructors, being courteous means much more than saying "Yes, sir" and "Yes, ma'am."

(4) While being polite is part of being courteous, it is not the word's essence. (5) In fact, you can be rude while being courteous. (6) Using an insolent tone of voice when you say "yes, sir" can mean the opposite of what the words indicate. (7) A sloppy bow can be ruder than no bow. (8) If you do not bow, the other person might excuse you because you are not used to formal manners.

(9) Part of becoming a martial artist is developing the proper attitude, which includes being courteous, respectful, and grateful. (10) *Courteous, respect,* and *grateful* are closely linked. (11) Being courteous is an attitude, not just empty words or rituals. (12) In a martial arts class, teachers are not the only instructors. (13) After all, my school is best. (14) You should respect the head instructor and his or her assistants. (15) More than that, though, anyone who helps you is a teacher. (16) Even a new student can teach you. (17) You won't learn a better technique from a new student, but <u>you may learn something else</u>. (18) When you learn something while explaining a concept to someone, that person has helped increase your knowledge. (19) Respect everyone, because

GO ON

you can learn something from anyone. Also, be grateful that other people
(20)
help you learn.

When you realize how *courteous* relates to *respect* and *gratefulness*, you
(21)
are on your way to improving your character.

Courteous behavior also helps you convince others to improve their
(22)
character. If others are discourteous but you continue to behave courteously,
(23)
your behavior may influence them to act in a more civilized manner.

Courtesy shows respect. Courteous behavior based on respect eases
(24)   (25)
social interaction and helps maintain good relations with other people.

Courtesy helps build character in a positive way.
(26)

1 **What should be added to BEST grab the readers' attention?**

  A a dictionary definition of *courteous*

  B a comparison of *courteous* and *discourteous*

  C a pertinent quotation

  D background information about the history of *courteous*

2 **Which sentence provides a clear thesis statement?**

  A Even small children at the school learn good manners.

  B Being courteous is also an attitude that influences behavior.

  C The word comes from a word that means "court."

  D Some people learn good manners from their parents.

3 **Which sentence would BEST follow sentence 6?**

  A The correct word choice shows that you're really being polite.

  B Many people think they don't have time to be polite.

  C Being polite helps make life easier for everyone.

  D A sneering look can also undermine courteous words.

4 **Which sentence should be added following sentence 8 to provide appropriate elaboration?**

  A However, a sloppy bow reveals that you know the proper etiquette but want to insult the other person.

  B Since we do not have royalty, we do not learn courtly manners.

  C We need to study the etiquette of other cultures.

  D Some people think that etiquette is old-fashioned.

5 Which sentence in paragraph 3 should be deleted to remove irrelevant details?

A   9   C   12

B   11   D   13

6 Which sentence should be added after sentence 15 to provide elaboration?

A   Most of us have had a teacher who helped in a very special way.

B   Too often the efforts of teachers are not appreciated.

C   This means that you may consider parents, siblings, friends, and even strangers to be teachers.

D   You yourself will eventually be a teacher because you will teach someone else what you have learned.

7 What is the BEST way to revise <u>you may learn something else</u> in sentence 17 to add supporting details?

A   maybe you will learn that or something else useful

B   you may learn something about character or self-discipline

C   other students in the class will probably learn from the new student

D   you may learn something important about life

8 Which sentence provides the BEST support to add after sentence 23?

A   At the very least, they will become aware of their incivility.

B   Discourtesy discourages some people.

C   People who behave discourteously usually have other character flaws.

D   Every generation tends to think that people are becoming rude.

9 Which sentence should be added after sentence 26 to help show how the extended definition differs from a dictionary definition?

A   Courteous behavior is not simply politeness or consideration.

B   Many martial arts schools teach their students the value of courtesy.

C   Road rage would not be a problem if people were courteous.

D   We need more books on the importance of courtesy.

10 Which sentence should be added to the end of the essay to show the relevance of this definition to other people?

A   If you try to be courteous, you may win an award.

B   We should all work on developing our character in positive ways.

C   If everyone worked to develop courteous behavior, there would be fewer conflicts of all kinds.

D   Taking martial arts is important because it helps students become more courteous.

for **COLLECTION 5**　*page 726*

Writing Workshop: Editorial

DIRECTIONS Roland is submitting an editorial about the school's closed lunch policy to his school newspaper. This rough draft of his paper contains errors in organization and development. Read the draft, and answer questions 1 through 10.

Lunchtime Freedom and Responsibility

Some school districts allow all high school students to leave campus (1) for lunch as long as they have their parents' permission. Only one high school in this district—ours—does not allow any students to leave campus (2) during lunchtime. Our high school is forced to pack us all into a too-small (3) cafeteria during our short lunch break. We need to do something about the (4) overcrowding.

Before they agreed to open-lunch privileges, administrators at Jackson (5) High School worried that students would speed back and forth to restaurants during the forty-five-minute break. When the administrators (6) allowed a trial period, students had no car accidents or injuries during their off-campus lunch hours. Once parents and administrators saw the results (7) of the trial period, they agreed to make the policy permanent.

Our cafeteria is so overcrowded that we often have to stand in line for (8) twenty to twenty-five minutes to buy lunch. Because our lunch break is (9) only forty-five minutes long, we often have to gobble down our food. Some (10) students even skip lunch because they don't have time to eat. One way to (11) ease this overcrowding would be to stagger lunch breaks, but that is not an option. Allowing seniors to eat off campus, when they have the permission (12) of their parents or guardians, would ease the overcrowding of the school cafeteria. The reduced cafeteria crowd would help the school district (13) avoid building a new, very expensive cafeteria in which to house us every noon hour.

GO ON

(14) Some administrators and community leaders have expressed concern that students might endanger themselves and others by speeding to and from the campus at lunchtime. (15) Our lunch break is only forty-five minutes long. (16) Open-lunch schools have not experienced an increase in accidents involving students off campus. (17) Some of those schools have lunch breaks the same length of time as ours or even shorter, but some allow an hour for lunch. (18) If we add ten minutes to the lunchtime break, we can decrease the probability that students will speed back to school after lunch.

(19) Allowing high school seniors to leave the campus for lunch would not only relieve overcrowding in the school cafeteria, but it would also give seniors a chance to show their responsibility. (20) By driving carefully and returning on time to their after-lunch classes, they can show that they deserve to be trusted. (21) We seniors are prepared to demonstrate our responsibility in a trial run.

1 What is the BEST sentence to add to grab readers' attention?

  A Lots of schools allow seniors to leave campus during lunch.

  B I think the school board should eliminate overcrowding.

  C Five percent—that's the percentage of high schools in our city that don't allow seniors to leave for lunch.

  D We seniors want to be able to leave campus at lunchtime so that we can get some decent food.

2 What is the BEST background information to add following sentence 1?

  A In the old days, there wasn't a cafeteria and most students brought their lunch to school.

  B Crowded school cafeterias led some schools to allow high school students to leave campus at lunch.

  C Most students want some variety in their lunches, so they don't want to eat in the cafeteria every day.

  D Some parents won't give permission, but other students shouldn't suffer just because those parents are strict.

GO ON

3 **What is the BEST way to revise sentence 4 to provide a clear opinion statement?**

A   Overcrowding is a serious problem and makes it impossible for students to enjoy a peaceful, unhurried lunch.

B   To prevent the spread of illness through the school, we should stop packing so many students into such a small space.

C   We can do something about the over-crowding if we all get together and discuss ways to solve the problem.

D   To help ease overcrowding in the cafeteria, seniors should be allowed to leave the campus for lunch.

4 **Which sentence provides the BEST evidence to follow sentence 6?**

A   Considering the number of students who drive to school, the number of accidents on the way to school is very small.

B   Also, local law enforcement officials received no reports of misbehavior during students' lunch hours off campus.

C   Administrators and parents were pleasantly surprised by these results.

D   The students showed that they could be responsible, and they were rewarded with more privileges.

5 **Which sentence should be added after sentence 7 to BEST address the counterargument mentioned in that paragraph?**

A   No serious problems have been reported at that high school since the open-lunch policy was adopted.

B   Of course, if problems develop, administrators can always change the policy again.

C   A longer lunch break might also help, because students wouldn't be in such a hurry to get back to class.

D   If our administrators have similar concerns, they should give us a trial period so that we can show that we're responsible.

6 **The organization of the essay would BEST be improved by moving paragraph 2 to—**

A   follow paragraph 3

B   follow paragraph 4

C   follow paragraph 5

D   precede paragraph 1

GO ON

7 **Which sentence provides the BEST support to follow sentence 11?**

A   That would be my second suggestion for solving the overcrowding, but administrators don't like that solution.

B   Another solution would be to provide more refrigerators and to have more students bring their lunches to school.

C   Administrators have ruled that staggering lunch breaks would complicate the scheduling of classes.

D   I think that cafeteria staff wouldn't want to work longer hours.

8 **Which factual evidence would BEST follow sentence 12?**

A   I'm sure that other students would be happy that fewer seniors would be standing in line with them.

B   Forty percent of seniors say they would eat off campus two or three times a week.

C   Seniors would be happier if they could eat somewhere other than the school cafeteria.

D   Some parents would prefer that their students go home to eat instead of eating in the cafeteria.

9 **Which sentence should be added after sentence 18 to provide a logical argument supporting Roland's position?**

A   Lengthening the school day by ten minutes is a small schedule adjustment to help ensure the safety of students.

B   I don't think ten minutes will make much difference, but it might persuade administrators.

C   If administrators decide against us, we seniors will feel mistreated.

D   My mother, for one, wants me to have a longer lunch break so that I can help her at home.

10 **What is the BEST call to action to add to the conclusion?**

A   Let's have more privileges to prepare us for adulthood.

B   If some seniors behave irresponsibly, the privilege can be taken away.

C   We've proved that we're responsible in other ways.

D   Let's work with administrators to implement a three-month trial run testing open-lunch privileges.

for **COLLECTION 6** | *page 824*

Writing Workshop: Analyzing Literature

DIRECTIONS The following is a rough draft of an essay analyzing a short story. It contains errors in development and organization. Some of the questions refer to numbered sentences within the text. Read the essay, and answer questions 1 through 10.

Satire in Dostoevsky's Story "The Crocodile"

(1) In Fyodor Dostoevsky's story, a crocodile on exhibit in a Petersburg arcade swallows the character Ivan Matveitch whole. (2) Instead of dying, however, Matveitch lives on inside the crocodile and interacts with the narrator and others. (3) These interactions help reveal the underlying purpose of Dostoevsky's story.

(4) The story explores the responses of various characters to the swallowing of Matveitch. (5) Readers might expect Matveitch's wife and friends to be grief-stricken and would expect concern, at least, from Matveitch's colleagues. (6) Similarly, readers might expect the crocodile's owner to react to the event with more concern for Matveitch than for the crocodile and its revenue-generating potential.

(7) However, no one reacts as expected. (8) Matveitch's wife, Elena Ivanovna, sees the event as an opportunity to free herself from her husband. (9) She seems almost hopeful that she will be widowed and, when Matveitch survives, begins thinking of grounds for divorce. (10) The narrator quickly grows bored with Matveitch's situation and flirts with Elena even as they leave the arcade; he later deeply resents Matveitch.

(11) Further, Matveitch's colleague, Timofey Semyonitch, suggests leaving Matveitch in the crocodile for as long as three months. (12) Semyonitch says that by staying in the crocodile, Matveitch can help attract capital to Russia and that economic principles are "paramount" in the situation because the crocodile is private property. (13) The crocodile's German owner has a similar response. (14) No one seriously intends to rescue Matveitch. (15) From within the

GO ON →

> crocodile, Matveitch himself holds trivial conversations with people outside. He becomes increasingly self-important and vain regarding his (16) new, special status. He also considers calling for others to join him inside (17) the crocodile.
>
> Dostoevsky thus uses "The Crocodile" to satirize human nature, (18) showing each character, including Matveitch, jockeying to gain as much as possible from the bureaucrat's situation. In the story, the narrator, (19) Elena Ivanovna, Timofey Semyonitch, and even Matveitch himself react to the apparent tragedy not by seeking Matveitch's rescue but by indulging their self-serving, pretentious, and petty impulses. Readers are implicitly (20) asked to compare the characters' concerns to the priorities we expect them to have. Even in the midst of tragedy, the story's characters remain (21) self-centered and trivial.

1 **Which sentence provides the BEST attention-grabbing opener?**

   A Fyodor Dostoevsky wrote novels and short stories.

   B Fyodor Dostoevsky is one of the greatest Russian writers.

   C How can an overfed crocodile help to satirize people and ideas?

   D "Those are crocodile's tears," muttered Timofey Semyonitch.

2 **What information should be added to sentence 1?**

   A the titles of several stories by Fyodor Dostoevsky

   B the story's title, "The Crocodile"

   C the name of the story's translator, Constance Garnett

   D the names of well-known scholars who study Dostoevsky

3 **How should sentence 3 be written to provide a clear thesis?**

   A These interactions help reveal the underlying purpose of Dostoevsky's story, to confuse and annoy readers.

   B These interactions help reveal the underlying purpose of Dostoevsky's story, to establish a dominant metaphor.

   C These interactions help reveal the underlying purpose of Dostoevsky's story, to explore the meaning of friendship.

   D These interactions help reveal the underlying purpose of Dostoevsky's story, to satirize human nature and society.

4 **Which sentence would BEST elaborate upon sentence 10?**

A   Like Elena Ivanovna, he is foolish.

B   He objects to having to attend to Matveitch's concerns and run errands for him.

C   His attitude shows readers that he is biased and cannot be a reliable narrator.

D   His resentment shows that he is used to having authority over Matveitch.

5 **Which sentence should be added at the end of the third paragraph to summarize a key point?**

A   The actions of both characters reveal their selfishness, greed, and shallowness.

B   Dostoevsky writes satire to make important points about flaws in Russian society.

C   Most of Dostoevsky's longer works subtly address common defects of character.

D   The characters' responses emphasize the economic confusion of nineteenth-century Russia.

6 **Which sentence provides the BEST textual evidence to be added after sentence 13?**

A   His sole concern is for his crocodile's health.

B   He worries about the same issues as Timofey Semyonitch.

C   His response helps prove that the story satirizes human nature.

D   He plans to increase his own income by putting the crocodile and Matveitch on display.

7 **What textual evidence would BEST follow sentence 16?**

A   Matveitch "expressed the desire" to view the crocodile on January 13, 1865.

B   The crocodile's room contains a number of cockatoos and a group of monkeys.

C   The crocodile's owner grows upset when he realizes that one of the visitors did not pay his entrance fees.

D   Matveitch speculates that he will be able to "scintillate" listeners and flirt harmlessly from within the crocodile.

8 **What elaboration would BEST follow sentence 17?**

A   His pride leads him to say that the narrator would get in, too, if he were "self-sacrificing enough."

B   His desire to inform others of his circumstances convinces him to describe conditions inside the crocodile.

C   His dependence on the kindness of others forces him to ask favors of his friend and colleague, the narrator.

D   His concerns about the economy drive him to wonder how much the crocodile's owner will charge for the crocodile.

9 **Which sentence should begin a new paragraph so that only one key point is discussed in each body paragraph?**

A   6   C   15

B   9   D   19

10 What is the BEST comment to add to the end of the essay to relate the analysis to life?

A Dostoevsky uses this story to teach a lesson and to inspire laughter.

B Dostoevsky asks readers to reject the vanity of his story's characters.

C Dostoevsky examines this theme in greater depth and detail in his other stories.

D Dostoevsky concludes that his characters have not learned any lessons from the story's central incident.

for **COLLECTION 7** page 1098

Writing Workshop: Reporting Literary Research

DIRECTIONS The following is a rough draft of a research paper about a literary work by Anton Shammas. The draft contains errors in development, organization, and format. Some of the questions refer to numbered sentences within the text. Answer questions 1 and 2. Then, read the essay, and answer questions 3 through 15.

1 **What is the BEST way for the writer to begin a research plan?**

  A List novels about life in the Middle East.

  B Check Internet encyclopedias for articles on this topic.

  C Consult general reference works to answer the *5W-How?* questions.

  D Call a literature professor at a state university, and ask for assistance.

2 **To BEST organize the results of the research, the writer should—**

  A list all the quotations to be included in the paper

  B add detailed source information to all research note cards

  C arrange research note cards according to each source's date of publication

  D create a detailed outline by arranging note cards by their main-idea headings

---

A Question of Identity

A person whose ethnic background conflicts with his or her nationality (1) may wrestle with questions of personal identity. Such questions of identity (2) surface in the Christian Israeli Palestinian author Anton Shammas's work.

In his novel *Arabesques*, elements of Shammas's ethnic and national identity (3) clash. Shammas in his novel reveals his personal struggle to discover his (4) own identity.

Arabesques' drifting plot resembles a meandering search for personal (5) identity. Looping narrative lines echo Shammas's attempts to disclose what (6) it is to be a Palestinian in Israel. The book is based on the author's experi- (7) ences while growing up in Israel. It also examines his relationships with (8) other Palestinians and a Jewish writer. The novel's narrator works to find (9) his place in society, as do various Jewish and Palestinian writers who struggle to "place" Palestinians. For example, Professor Edward Said, a (10) well-known Palestinian, titled his own memoir *Out of Place*. Similarly, (11)

GO ON

David Grossman in *The Yellow Wind* and *Sleeping on a Wire* examines the

position of Palestinians living in the state of Israel. Journalist Yoram Binur
(12)
examines this struggle for identity by disguising himself as an Arab. Even
(13)
Shammas's title, *Arabesques*, reflects the author's search for identity: An

arabesque is a complex design made of intertwined lines. Metaphorically,
(14)
arabesque threads symbolize the interwoven threads of the novel's plot.

While *Arabesques* examines issues of identity, it remains a poetic novel.
(15)
Shammas worked with translator Vivian Eden to ensure that the English
(16)
translation would be true to the spirit of the Hebrew original. The result of
(17)
their work is a translation filled with highly poetic language. Shammas
(18)
creates descriptions so vivid that they play in the reader's mind like bright

film clips illuminating the narrator's experiences.

Shammas's poetic narrator often speaks ironically, as might be
(19)
expected of a Palestinian author who, as a Christian in Israel, is a minority

within a minority. Although he is home, Shammas is, like Said, ironically
(20)
"out of place." Said himself lived in several countries. Some of *Arabesques'*
(21)   (22)
subtlest ironies lie in its allusions to historical events and biblical narratives.

As a Christian Arab, the narrator Anton straddles the worlds of both
(23)
Israeli Palestinians and Israeli Jews while maintaining his identity as

a Christian.

The complexity of Shammas's struggle for personal identity is further
(24)
revealed by the ironic narrator's unreliability and confusion. For example,
(25)
the narrator relates a heart-wrenchingly ironic tale: A Jewish infant is stolen

from his mother, who is told that the child has died, and the child is given

to a childless Arab family. Just as ironically, the book's narrator reveals that
(26)
he intended to use a Japanese—not Palestinian or Israeli—saying that he

once heard in a movie as the book's motto. He then admits to being
(27)
unreliable, telling readers that the movie's director had made up the

GO ON

"saying" altogether. With equal irony, the narrator describes his family (28) history as an Arab soap opera, a description that undermines the novel's somber tone. This use of an unreliable narrator encourages readers to pay (29) close attention to Shammas's struggle for personal identity.

Using irony, poetic language, and an unreliable narrator, *Arabesques* is (30) interesting in several ways. Shammas examines the complex personal (31) identity of a Christian Palestinian living in the state of Israel. Many readers (32) will feel, after reading this book, a greater empathy with people like Shammas, people marginalized by the culture of the majority.

Works Cited

Shammas, Anton. *Arabesques*. Trans. Vivian Eden. New York: Harper, 1989.

Binur, Yoram. *My Enemy, My Self*. Trans. Uriel Grunfeld. New York:

   Penguin, 1990.

Said, Edward W. *Out of Place: A Memoir*. New York: Vintage, 1999.

Grossman, David. *Sleeping on a Wire: Conversations with Palestinians in Israel*.

   Trans. Haim Watzman. New York: Farrar, 1993.

- - -. *The Yellow Wind*. Trans. Haim Watzman. London: Pan, 1989.

---

3 **What is the BEST opening to add to the beginning of the essay?**

A a definition of irony

B information about the author's works

C an interesting hook to get the reader's attention

D statistics about the number of novels written in Hebrew

4 **What type of background information would BEST be added after sentence 2?**

A descriptions of various groups of immigrants

B a short history of Israel and the people of the Middle East

C information about political processes and groups in the state of Israel

D an explanation of why identity is especially problematic for Israeli Palestinians

5 **Which phrase should be added to the beginning of sentence 4 to make the thesis statement clearer?**

A   As a respected poet and professor in the United States for many years,

B   Similar to his compatriot, Sayed Kashua, who also published in Hebrew,

C   Using a drifting plot, poetic language, and an ironic and unreliable narrator,

D   With a narrative style that is often as confusing as that of Laurence Sterne,

6 **Where should sentence 13 be moved to maintain logical order?**

A   before sentence 7

B   before sentence 18

C   before sentence 26

D   before sentence 29

7 **What details should be added following sentence 18 to develop paragraph 3?**

A   examples of the novel's poetic language

B   background information about the translator

C   translations of passages from some of Shammas's poems

D   side-by-side comparisons of the Hebrew and English text

8 **Which sentence should be deleted because it includes an irrelevant detail?**

A   17   C   29

B   21   D   31

9 **What kind of supporting evidence would BEST follow sentence 22?**

A   a comparison of the narrator with Palestinian narrators of similar novels

B   a description of the countryside and larger towns around Shammas's village

C   a list of the articles and books that Shammas published in Arabic, Hebrew, and English

D   an analysis of an ironic allusion to a historical event or biblical narrative

10 **Which details should be added after sentence 25?**

A   He shows his command of the narrative by evoking the reader's sympathy.

B   The narrator says that he made up the infant's story yet later suggests it might be true.

C   His descriptions of life within his family are usually humorous, but they are sometimes sad.

D   This narrator reminds me of the narrator of Laurence Sterne's *The Life and Opinions of Tristram Shandy, Gentleman.*

11 **Which information should be added to the end of sentence 27?**

A   a Palestinian saying

B   a summary of the movie's plot

C   a description of a similar movie

D   a parenthetical citation to this page of the novel

GO ON

12 What kind of support would BEST be added after sentence 28?

A examples from the novel showing how Shammas's family history resembles a soap opera

B an example from the novel that shows Shammas being mistaken for an Israeli Jew

C a description of the narrator's various plans for the novel he intends to write

D a sentence in which the narrator describes the members of his family

13 Which phrase would BEST be added to the beginning of sentence 31 to restate the thesis?

A Exploring his own internal ethnic conflict,

B Revealing the thinking of a very talented writer,

C Using the English language to reach a wide audience,

D Showing a different aspect of Arab culture and family life,

14 Which sentence should be added to the end of the essay as a final insight?

A It is ironic and revealing that Shammas has been living in the United States.

B Unfortunately, it is sometimes difficult to locate English translations of Shammas's poems.

C Shammas's message is universal: We all undergo similar struggles to find out who we are.

D For another perspective on this topic, read Sayed Kashua's *Dancing Arabs*, also published in Hebrew.

15 What major change needs to be made to the Works Cited list?

A Change all titles to boldface.

B Put the entries in alphabetical order.

C Delete the periods following each entry.

D Add an author to the entry for *The Yellow Wind*.

Answer Sheet 1

Collection __________

Writing Workshop

1	Ⓐ	Ⓑ	Ⓒ	Ⓓ	**5**	Ⓐ	Ⓑ	Ⓒ	Ⓓ	**8**	Ⓐ Ⓑ Ⓒ Ⓓ
2	Ⓐ	Ⓑ	Ⓒ	Ⓓ	**6**	Ⓐ	Ⓑ	Ⓒ	Ⓓ	**9**	Ⓐ Ⓑ Ⓒ Ⓓ
3	Ⓐ	Ⓑ	Ⓒ	Ⓓ	**7**	Ⓐ	Ⓑ	Ⓒ	Ⓓ	**10**	Ⓐ Ⓑ Ⓒ Ⓓ
4	Ⓐ	Ⓑ	Ⓒ	Ⓓ							

Answer Sheet 2

Collection _________

Writing Workshop

1 Ⓐ Ⓑ Ⓒ Ⓓ	6 Ⓐ Ⓑ Ⓒ Ⓓ	11 Ⓐ Ⓑ Ⓒ Ⓓ
2 Ⓐ Ⓑ Ⓒ Ⓓ	7 Ⓐ Ⓑ Ⓒ Ⓓ	12 Ⓐ Ⓑ Ⓒ Ⓓ
3 Ⓐ Ⓑ Ⓒ Ⓓ	8 Ⓐ Ⓑ Ⓒ Ⓓ	13 Ⓐ Ⓑ Ⓒ Ⓓ
4 Ⓐ Ⓑ Ⓒ Ⓓ	9 Ⓐ Ⓑ Ⓒ Ⓓ	14 Ⓐ Ⓑ Ⓒ Ⓓ
5 Ⓐ Ⓑ Ⓒ Ⓓ	10 Ⓐ Ⓑ Ⓒ Ⓓ	15 Ⓐ Ⓑ Ⓒ Ⓓ

Answer Key

Collection 1

Reflective Essay

p. 3

1. C (attention-grabbing opening)
2. B (background information)
3. D (experience's significance)
4. A (effective organization)
5. B (relevant details)
6. C (descriptive details)
7. C (transitional words)
8. A (narrative details)
9. B (writer's thoughts and feelings)
10. D (insight about life)

Collection 2

Problem-Solution Essay

p. 6

1. B (attention-grabbing opening)
2. C (background information)
3. D (thesis statement)
4. B (effective organization)
5. C (elaboration)
6. A (main idea)
7. D (addressing counterarguments)
8. B (supporting evidence)
9. C (summary of key points)
10. A (call to action)

Collection 3

Persuasive Essay

p. 10

1. C (background information)
2. B (hint at solution)
3. B (effective organization)
4. D (supporting evidence)
5. B (ethical appeal)
6. A (elaboration)
7. C (logical appeal)
8. D (elaboration)
9. C (addressing a counterclaim)
10. A (call to action)

Collection 4

Extended Definition

p. 14

1. C (attention-grabbing opening)
2. B (thesis)
3. D (elaboration)
4. A (elaboration)
5. D (relevant details)
6. C (elaboration)
7. B (supporting details)
8. A (supporting evidence)
9. A (distinguishing from dictionary definition)
10. C (relevance of definition)

Collection 5

Editorial

p. 16

1. C (attention-grabbing opening)
2. B (background information)
3. D (opinion statement)
4. B (specific evidence)
5. D (addressing counterargument)
6. B (effective organization)
7. C (supporting evidence)
8. B (factual evidence)
9. A (logical argument)
10. D (call to action)

Collection 6

Literary Analysis

p. 20

1. C (attention-grabbing opener)
2. B (author and title of story)
3. D (thesis statement)
4. B (elaboration)
5. A (key points)
6. D (evidence)
7. D (evidence)
8. A (elaboration)
9. C (organization)
10. B (insight about life)

Collection 7

Literary Research Paper

p. 24

1. C (research plan)
2. D (organizing)
3. C (interesting opening)
4. D (background information)
5. C (clear thesis statement)
6. A (organization)
7. A (elaboration)
8. B (relevant details)
9. D (supporting evidence)
10. B (elaboration)
11. D (citation)
12. A (supporting example)
13. A (restatement of thesis)
14. C (final insight)
15. B (citation)

Workshop Scales and Rubrics

        ANALYTICAL SCALE

Writing: Reflective Essay

Use the chart below to evaluate a reflective essay. Circle the numbers that best indicate how well the criteria are met. With these nine criteria, the lowest possible score is 0, the highest 36.

4 = Clearly meets this criterion

3 = Makes a serious effort to meet this criterion and is fairly successful

2 = Makes some effort to meet this criterion but with little success

1 = Does not achieve this criterion

0 = Unscorable

CRITERIA FOR EVALUATION	RATING
Genre, Organization, and Focus	
Introduction includes an engaging opening.	4 3 2 1
Introduction hints at significance of personal experience.	4 3 2 1
Descriptive details bring each event to life.	4 3 2 1
Order of events is clear.	4 3 2 1
Essay vividly describes the defining moment of the experience.	4 3 2 1
Conclusion reveals the effect of the experience on the writer.	4 3 2 1
Conclusion offers a direct connection between the experience and an insight about life.	4 3 2 1
Language Conventions	
Standard English spelling, punctuation, capitalization, and manuscript form are used appropriately for this grade level.	4 3 2 1
Standard English sentence and paragraph structure, grammar, usage, and diction are used appropriately for this grade level.	4 3 2 1
Total Points:	

Writing: Reflective Essay

CRITERIA FOR EVALUATION	SCORE POINT 4	SCORE POINT 3	SCORE POINT 2	SCORE POINT 1
Genre, Organization, and Focus				
Introduction includes an engaging opening.	Introduction grabs readers' attention with an interesting anecdote, fact, or quotation.	Introduction interests readers but does not grab their attention.	Introduction is only partially successful at engaging readers' attention.	Introduction lacks an engaging opening and does not interest readers.
Introduction hints at significance of personal experience.	Introduction gives specific and detailed hints about the significance of the experience.	Introduction broadly describes the significance of the experience.	Introduction gives vague hints about the significance of the experience.	The significance of the experience is missing or is unrelated to the experience.
Descriptive details bring each event to life.	Relevant, richly detailed descriptions bring events to life.	Descriptive details relate events.	Essay includes few or irrelevant details about events.	Description of events is minimal or missing.
Order of events is clear.	Order of events is clear and in logical order with transitional words to indicate changes in time.	Events are related mostly in logical order.	Some events are related in logical order, while other events seem out of place.	Order of events is unclear, or events are ordered randomly.
Essay vividly describes the defining moment of the experience.	Precise, descriptive language reveals defining moment and brings it to life for the reader.	Essay uses some descriptive language to reveal defining moment.	Defining moment of experience is confusingly and/or vaguely described.	Essay omits defining moment of experience.
Conclusion reveals the effect of the experience on the writer.	Conclusion intrigues readers by clearly and specifically stating experience's effect on the writer.	Conclusion clearly describes the experience's effect on the writer.	Effect of the experience on the writer is addressed in a confusing manner.	Experience's effect on the writer is missing.
Conclusion offers a direct connection between the experience and an insight about life.	Conclusion specifically reflects on what was learned or what changed because of the experience, clearly revealing the experience's significance.	Conclusion generally reflects on what was learned or what changed because of the experience and reveals its significance.	Conclusion's statement of the experience's significance seems unrelated to the essay.	Conclusion omits any reference to the significance of the experience.

ANALYTICAL SCORING RUBRIC

CRITERIA FOR EVALUATION	SCORE POINT 4	SCORE POINT 3	SCORE POINT 2	SCORE POINT 1
Language Conventions				
Standard English spelling, punctuation, capitalization, and manuscript form are used appropriately for this grade level.	Standard English spelling, punctuation, capitalization, and manuscript form are used appropriately for this grade level throughout the essay.	Standard English spelling, punctuation, capitalization, and manuscript form are used appropriately for this grade level, with few problems.	Inconsistent use of standard English spelling, punctuation, capitalization, and manuscript form disrupts readers' comprehension.	Minimal use of standard English spelling, punctuation, capitalization, and manuscript form confuses readers.
Standard English sentence and paragraph structure, grammar, usage, and diction are used appropriately for this grade level.	Standard English sentence and paragraph structure, grammar, usage, and diction are used appropriately for this grade level throughout the essay.	Standard English sentence and paragraph structure, grammar, usage, and diction are used appropriately for this grade level, with few problems.	Inconsistent use of standard English sentence and paragraph structure, grammar, usage, and diction disrupts readers' comprehension.	Minimal use of standard English sentence and paragraph structure, grammar, usage, and diction confuses readers.

Writing: Problem-Solution Essay

Use the chart below to evaluate a problem-solution essay. Circle the numbers that best indicate how well the criteria are met. With these ten criteria, the lowest possible score is 0, the highest 40.

4 = Clearly meets this criterion

3 = Makes a serious effort to meet this criterion and is fairly successful

2 = Makes some effort to meet this criterion but with little success

1 = Does not achieve this criterion

0 = Unscorable

CRITERIA FOR EVALUATION	RATING
Genre, Organization, and Focus	
Introduction grabs readers' attention.	4 3 2 1
Background information is provided where necessary.	4 3 2 1
Thesis statement identifies problem and best solution.	4 3 2 1
Problem is analyzed in essay's body.	4 3 2 1
Reasons and evidence support proposed solution.	4 3 2 1
Essay addresses objections and counterarguments.	4 3 2 1
Conclusion includes call to action.	4 3 2 1
Conclusion restates thesis in a compelling way.	4 3 2 1
Language Conventions	
Standard English spelling, punctuation, capitalization, and manuscript form are used appropriately for this grade level.	4 3 2 1
Standard English sentence and paragraph structure, grammar, usage, and diction are used appropriately for this grade level.	4 3 2 1
Total Points:	

Writing: Problem-Solution Essay

CRITERIA FOR EVALUATION	SCORE POINT 4	SCORE POINT 3	SCORE POINT 2	SCORE POINT 1
▶ **Genre, Organization, and Focus**				
Introduction grabs readers' attention.	Engaging introduction grabs readers' attention with an interesting anecdote or example.	Introduction interests readers.	Introduction is dull or unrelated to essay's purpose.	Introduction is missing.
Background information is provided where necessary.	Background information necessary for understanding problem is provided.	Most background information necessary for understanding problem is provided.	Some sketchy background information is provided.	No useful background information is provided.
Thesis statement identifies problem and best solution.	Thesis statement clearly presents the problem and explicitly states the proposed solution.	Thesis statement presents the problem and the essay's focus.	Thesis statement is confusing and hard to follow.	Thesis statement is missing.
Problem is analyzed in essay's body.	Clear, relevant, and detailed analysis breaks problem into its constituent elements.	General analysis breaks problem into its constituent elements.	Confusing analysis or general discussion focuses on problem.	Analysis of the problem is missing.
Reasons and evidence support proposed solution.	Sound logical reasons and solid evidence support proposed solution.	Generally logical reasons and occasionally weak evidence support proposed solution.	Unclear or confusing reasons and weak evidence support proposed solution.	Reasons and evidence are missing or are unrelated to the proposed solution.
Essay addresses objections and counterarguments.	Realistic objections and counter-arguments are clearly and success-fully addressed.	Realistic objections and counter-arguments are addressed.	Objections and counterarguments are not realistic or are addressed in a confusing manner.	Objections and counterarguments are not addressed.

for **COLLECTION 2**   **page 330**   *continued*   **ANALYTICAL SCORING RUBRIC**

CRITERIA FOR EVALUATION	SCORE POINT 4	SCORE POINT 3	SCORE POINT 2	SCORE POINT 1
Conclusion includes call to action.	Clear and explicit call to action suggests immediate steps to implement solution and identifies participants.	Call to action suggests steps to implement solution.	Call to action is unclear or confusing.	Call to action is missing.
Conclusion restates thesis in a compelling way.	Conclusion freshly restates thesis, inspiring confidence in solution.	Conclusion clearly restates thesis.	Conclusion restates thesis but is confusing or identical to its statement in the introduction.	Conclusion does not restate thesis.

Language Conventions

CRITERIA FOR EVALUATION	SCORE POINT 4	SCORE POINT 3	SCORE POINT 2	SCORE POINT 1
Standard English spelling, punctuation, capitalization, and manuscript form are used appropriately for this grade level.	Standard English spelling, punctuation, capitalization, and manuscript form are used appropriately for this grade level throughout the essay.	Standard English spelling, punctuation, capitalization, and manuscript form are used appropriately for this grade level, with few problems.	Inconsistent use of standard English spelling, punctuation, capitalization, and manuscript form disrupts readers' comprehension.	Minimal use of standard English spelling, punctuation, capitalization, and manuscript form confuses readers.
Standard English sentence and paragraph structure, grammar, usage, and diction are used appropriately for this grade level.	Standard English sentence and paragraph structure, grammar, usage, and diction are used appropriately for this grade level throughout the essay.	Standard English sentence and paragraph structure, grammar, usage, and diction are used appropriately for this grade level, with few problems.	Inconsistent use of standard English sentence and paragraph structure, grammar, usage, and diction disrupts readers' comprehension.	Minimal use of standard English sentence and paragraph structure, grammar, usage, and diction confuses readers.

                                    ANALYTICAL SCALE

Listening and Speaking: Presenting and Evaluating a Persuasive Speech

Use the chart below to assess students' presentations and evaluations of persuasive speeches. Circle the numbers that best indicate how well the criteria are met. With these nine criteria, the lowest possible score is 0, the highest 36.

4 = Clearly meets this criterion

3 = Makes a serious effort to meet this criterion and is fairly successful

2 = Makes some effort to meet this criterion but with little success

1 = Does not achieve this criterion

0 = Unscorable

CRITERIA FOR EVALUATION	RATING
The Speaker: Content, Organization, and Delivery	
Clear position statement presents speaker's opinion about problem and the best solution.	4 3 2 1
Reasons, such as evidence and appeals to logic, emotion, and ethics, support proposed solution.	4 3 2 1
Speech uses a deductive or inductive approach.	4 3 2 1
Reasons are presented in order of importance, from least to most important.	4 3 2 1
Speech uses rhetorical devices, such as repetition, rhetorical questions, and restatement.	4 3 2 1
Speaker presents arguments with effective delivery techniques.	4 3 2 1
The Listener	
Listener identifies appropriate use of appeals to logic, emotions, or ethics.	4 3 2 1
Listener distinguishes use of fallacious reasoning or propaganda (overgeneralization, false causality, bandwagon effect, or attack *ad hominem*).	4 3 2 1
Language Conventions	
Standard English grammar, usage, and diction are used appropriately for this grade level.	4 3 2 1
Total Points:	

for **COLLECTION 3**   *page 472*   **ANALYTICAL SCALE**

Writing: Persuasive Essay

Use the chart below to evaluate a persuasive essay. Circle the numbers that best indicate how well the criteria are met. With these ten criteria, the lowest possible score is 0, the highest 40.

4 = Clearly meets this criterion

3 = Makes a serious effort to meet this criterion and is fairly successful

2 = Makes some effort to meet this criterion but with little success

1 = Does not achieve this criterion

0 = Unscorable

WORKSHOP SCALES AND RUBRICS

CRITERIA FOR EVALUATION	RATING
Genre, Organization, and Focus	
Essay begins with striking statement or anecdote.	4 3 2 1
Introduction provides background information where necessary.	4 3 2 1
Introduction includes opinion statement that hints at the call to action.	4 3 2 1
Evidence and persuasive appeals support analysis of problem's causes and effects.	4 3 2 1
Specific call to action is proposed in conclusion.	4 3 2 1
Conclusion addresses counterclaims and objections to the call to action.	4 3 2 1
Conclusion restates opinion on situation and the need for change.	4 3 2 1
Essay ends with final call for action.	4 3 2 1
Language Conventions	
Standard English spelling, punctuation, capitalization, and manuscript form are used appropriately for this grade level.	4 3 2 1
Standard English sentence and paragraph structure, grammar, usage, and diction are used appropriately for this grade level.	4 3 2 1
Total Points:	

Writing: Persuasive Essay

CRITERIA FOR EVALUATION	SCORE POINT 4	SCORE POINT 3	SCORE POINT 2	SCORE POINT 1
Genre, Organization, and Focus				
Essay begins with striking statement or anecdote.	Introduction grabs readers' attention with a striking statement or intriguing anecdote.	Introduction attempts to interest readers.	Introduction is bland or dull.	Introduction is missing.
Introduction provides background information where necessary.	Introduction provides background information necessary to understanding the situation.	Most background information necessary to understanding the situation is provided.	Some sketchy background information is provided.	No useful background information is provided.
Introduction includes opinion statement that hints at the call to action.	Introduction includes clear, strong opinion statement that hints at the call to action.	Introduction includes opinion statement that hints at the call to action.	Introduction contains vague opinion statement and call to action.	Introduction contains no opinion statement.
Evidence and persuasive appeals support analysis of problem's causes and effects.	Credible evidence and solid persuasive appeals effectively support the problem's analysis.	Evidence and persuasive appeals support the problem's analysis.	Weak evidence and ineffective persuasive appeals loosely support the problem's analysis.	Evidence and persuasive appeals do not support the problem's analysis.
Specific call to action is proposed in conclusion.	Conclusion proposes clear, direct, and specific course of action.	Conclusion proposes course of action.	Proposed course of action is unclear and confusing.	Call to action is missing.
Conclusion addresses counterclaims and objections to the call to action.	Conclusion effectively and convincingly addresses readers' counterclaims and objections.	Conclusion somewhat effectively addresses readers' counterclaims and objections.	Conclusion weakly or ineffectively attempts to address readers' counterclaims and objections.	Conclusion makes no attempt to address readers' counterclaims and objections.

for **COLLECTION 3** `page 472` *continued*　　　　　　　　**ANALYTICAL SCORING RUBRIC**

WORKSHOP SCALES AND RUBRICS

CRITERIA FOR EVALUATION	SCORE POINT 4	SCORE POINT 3	SCORE POINT 2	SCORE POINT 1
Conclusion restates opinion on situation and the need for change.	Conclusion clearly restates opinion on situation and effectively communicates the need for change.	Conclusion restates opinion on situation and communicates the need for change.	Conclusion hints at opinion on situation and suggests the need for change.	Conclusion fails to restate opinion or to communicate the need for change.
Essay ends with final call for action.	Essay ends with highly motivating appeal for effective action.	Essay ends with clear appeal for action.	Essay ends with vague appeal for action.	Final call for action is missing.

Language Conventions

CRITERIA FOR EVALUATION	SCORE POINT 4	SCORE POINT 3	SCORE POINT 2	SCORE POINT 1
Standard English spelling, punctuation, capitalization, and manuscript form are used appropriately for this grade level.	Standard English spelling, punctuation, capitalization, and manuscript form are used appropriately for this grade level throughout the essay.	Standard English spelling, punctuation, capitalization, and manuscript form are used appropriately for this grade level, with few problems.	Inconsistent use of standard English spelling, punctuation, capitalization, and manuscript form disrupts readers' comprehension.	Minimal use of standard English spelling, punctuation, capitalization, and manuscript form confuses readers.
Standard English sentence and paragraph structure, grammar, usage, and diction are used appropriately for this grade level.	Standard English sentence and paragraph structure, grammar, usage, and diction are used appropriately for this grade level throughout the essay.	Standard English sentence and paragraph structure, grammar, usage, and diction are used appropriately for this grade level, with few problems.	Inconsistent use of standard English sentence and paragraph structure, grammar, usage, and diction disrupts readers' comprehension.	Minimal use of standard English sentence and paragraph structure, grammar, usage, and diction confuses readers.

Listening and Speaking: Giving a Persuasive Speech

Use the chart below to evaluate a persuasive speech adapted from a cause-and-effect essay. Circle the numbers that best indicate how well the criteria are met. With these nine criteria, the lowest possible score is 0, the highest 36.

4 = Clearly meets this criterion

3 = Makes a serious effort to meet this criterion and is fairly successful

2 = Makes some effort to meet this criterion but with little success

1 = Does not achieve this criterion

0 = Unscorable

CRITERIA FOR EVALUATION	RATING
Content, Organization, and Delivery	
Opener grabs audience's attention using an anecdote, a quotation, or an expert opinion.	4 3 2 1
Logical reasoning and evidence support the opinion statement.	4 3 2 1
Speech uses effective rhetorical devices, such as emotional, logical, and ethical appeals.	4 3 2 1
Speech addresses counterclaims and objections to opinion statement.	4 3 2 1
Conclusion includes a call to action.	4 3 2 1
Conclusion ends with a stirring final sentence.	4 3 2 1
Cause-and-effect essay is effectively adapted to speech that uses formal tone but relatively simple vocabulary, sentence structure, and logic.	4 3 2 1
Speaker uses effective delivery techniques to present arguments.	4 3 2 1
Language Conventions	
Standard English grammar, usage, and diction are used appropriately for this grade level.	4 3 2 1
Total Points:	

Writing: Extended Definition

Use the chart below to evaluate an extended definition. Circle the numbers that best indicate how well the criteria are met. With these nine criteria, the lowest possible score is 0, the highest 36.

4 = Clearly meets this criterion

3 = Makes a serious effort to meet this criterion and is fairly successful

2 = Makes some effort to meet this criterion but with little success

1 = Does not achieve this criterion

0 = Unscorable

WORKSHOP SCALES AND RUBRICS

CRITERIA FOR EVALUATION	RATING
Genre, Organization, and Focus	
Introduction includes a striking example, quotation, or question.	4 3 2 1
Introduction provides dictionary or common definition of word.	4 3 2 1
Thesis statement explains writer's take on definition.	4 3 2 1
Each example, description, anecdote, opinion, or comparison supports thesis.	4 3 2 1
Support is listed in clear and logical order.	4 3 2 1
Conclusion offers an overview or summary of definition.	4 3 2 1
Conclusion provides an explanation of the definition's importance or relevance to others.	4 3 2 1
Language Conventions	
Standard English spelling, punctuation, capitalization, and manuscript form are used appropriately for this grade level.	4 3 2 1
Standard English sentence and paragraph structure, grammar, usage, and diction are used appropriately for this grade level.	4 3 2 1
Total Points:	

Writing: Extended Definition

CRITERIA FOR EVALUATION	SCORE POINT 4	SCORE POINT 3	SCORE POINT 2	SCORE POINT 1
▶ **Genre, Organization, and Focus**				
Introduction includes a striking example, quotation, or question.	Introduction grabs readers' attention with a striking example, quotation, or question.	Introduction attempts to grab readers' attention.	Introduction's attention grabber is vague or dull.	Introduction's attention grabber is missing.
Introduction provides dictionary or common definition of word.	Introduction includes brief but specific dictionary definition.	Introduction provides general or vague definition of word.	Introduction provides partial definition of word.	Introduction provides inaccurate definition, or definition is missing.
Thesis statement explains writer's take on definition.	Thesis clearly identifies writer's main point about word.	Thesis hints at writer's main point about word.	Thesis is unclear or contains vague point about word.	Thesis is missing or omits writer's main point about word.
Examples, descriptions, anecdotes, opinions, and/or comparisons support thesis.	Clear and relevant examples, descriptions, anecdotes, opinions, and/or comparisons strongly support thesis.	Mostly clear examples, descriptions, anecdotes, opinions, and comparisons support thesis.	Support for the thesis is often weak, unclear, or irrelevant.	Support for the thesis is missing.
Support is listed in clear and logical order.	Support is in clear, logical order and uses new paragraphs for each new item or category; support includes transitional words or phrases when necessary.	Support is in logical order, but use of needed transitional words and phrases is limited, or paragraphing may be clumsy.	Some support is out of order, or order of support is confusing.	Support is ordered randomly.
Conclusion offers an overview or summary of definition.	Conclusion includes a clear and accurate overview or summary of definition.	Conclusion offers a vague but accurate overview or summary of definition.	Conclusion restates only the dictionary definition, or the definition's overview or summary is inaccurate.	Conclusion does not provide an overview or summary of the definition.

for **COLLECTION 4** **page 570** *continued*   **ANALYTICAL SCORING RUBRIC**

CRITERIA FOR EVALUATION	SCORE POINT 4	SCORE POINT 3	SCORE POINT 2	SCORE POINT 1
Conclusion provides an explanation of the definition's importance or relevance to others.	Conclusion convincingly explains why the extended definition is important or relevant to others.	Conclusion includes writer's opinion as to why definition should be important or relevant to others.	Conclusion hints at why the definition is important or relevant to others.	Conclusion fails to explain why the definition is important or relevant to others.

Language Conventions

CRITERIA FOR EVALUATION	SCORE POINT 4	SCORE POINT 3	SCORE POINT 2	SCORE POINT 1
Standard English spelling, punctuation, capitalization, and manuscript form are used appropriately for this grade level.	Standard English spelling, punctuation, capitalization, and manuscript form are used appropriately for this grade level throughout the definition.	Standard English spelling, punctuation, capitalization, and manuscript form are used appropriately for this grade level, with few problems.	Inconsistent use of standard English spelling, punctuation, capitalization, and manuscript form disrupts readers' comprehension.	Minimal use of standard English spelling, punctuation, capitalization, and manuscript form confuses readers.
Standard English sentence and paragraph structure, grammar, usage, and diction are used appropriately for this grade level.	Standard English sentence and paragraph structure, grammar, usage, and diction are used appropriately for this grade level throughout the definition.	Standard English sentence and paragraph structure, grammar, usage, and diction are used appropriately for this grade level, with few problems.	Inconsistent use of standard English sentence and paragraph structure, grammar, usage, and diction disrupts readers' comprehension.	Minimal use of standard English sentence and paragraph structure, grammar, usage, and diction confuses readers.

NAME ______ CLASS ______ DATE ______

for COLLECTION 5 **page 726** — ANALYTICAL SCALE

Writing: Editorial

Use the chart below to evaluate an editorial that examines a controversial issue. Circle the numbers that best indicate how well the criteria are met. With these ten criteria, the lowest possible score is 0, the highest 40.

4 = Clearly meets this criterion

3 = Makes a serious effort to meet this criterion and is fairly successful

2 = Makes some effort to meet this criterion but with little success

1 = Does not achieve this criterion

0 = Unscorable

CRITERIA FOR EVALUATION	RATING
Genre, Organization, and Focus	
Introduction interests readers with a surprising fact, statistic, or quotation.	4 3 2 1
Background information on issue is provided where necessary.	4 3 2 1
Introduction includes a position statement.	4 3 2 1
Facts and arguments support position.	4 3 2 1
Support is in logical order.	4 3 2 1
Editorial addresses counterarguments to position.	4 3 2 1
Conclusion restates writer's position on issue.	4 3 2 1
Conclusion ends with a call to action or an appeal for others to agree with position.	4 3 2 1
Language Conventions	
Standard English spelling, punctuation, capitalization, and manuscript form are used appropriately for this grade level.	4 3 2 1
Standard English sentence and paragraph structure, grammar, usage, and diction are used appropriately for this grade level.	4 3 2 1
Total Points:	

WORKSHOP SCALES AND RUBRICS

for **COLLECTION 5** *page 726* **ANALYTICAL SCORING RUBRIC**

Writing: Editorial

CRITERIA FOR EVALUATION	SCORE POINT 4	SCORE POINT 3	SCORE POINT 2	SCORE POINT 1
Genre, Organization, and Focus				
Introduction interests readers with a surprising fact, statistic, or quotation.	An interesting fact, statistic, or quotation grabs readers' attention.	Introduction generally interests readers.	Introduction is vague or unrelated to editorial's purpose.	Introduction is missing.
Background information on issue is provided where necessary.	Introduction offers relevant background information about issue.	Introduction gives some background information about issue.	Introduction gives insufficient or irrelevant background information.	No background information is provided.
Introduction includes a position statement.	Introduction clearly states writer's position on issue.	Position statement in introduction is somewhat general.	Position statement is weak or not specific to the issue.	Introduction omits position statement.
Facts and arguments support position.	Clear, relevant facts and arguments support position.	General facts and arguments appear to support position.	Confusing or irrelevant facts and arguments are used to support position.	Facts and arguments to support the position are not included.
Support is in logical order.	Supporting arguments are logically organized, most likely in order of importance.	Support is generally organized, with only minor lapses.	Supporting arguments appear to be organized haphazardly with significant logical gaps.	Supporting arguments are either missing or organized randomly.
Editorial addresses counterarguments to position.	Effective counterarguments are successfully addressed.	Effective counterarguments are somewhat effectively addressed.	Counterarguments are weak or are addressed in confusing manner.	Counterarguments are not addressed.

for **COLLECTION 5** `page 726` *continued*   **ANALYTICAL SCORING RUBRIC**

CRITERIA FOR EVALUATION	SCORE POINT 4	SCORE POINT 3	SCORE POINT 2	SCORE POINT 1
Conclusion restates writer's position on issue.	Conclusion clearly and freshly restates position.	Conclusion offers a general restatement of position.	Conclusion's restatement of position is unclear or repeats position statement from introduction.	Conclusion does not restate position.
Conclusion ends with a call to action or an appeal for others to agree with position.	Conclusion offers a specific call to action that tells readers what they can do about the issue or rallies readers to adopt the writer's position.	Conclusion ends with a broad call to action or somewhat encourages solidarity with writer's position.	Conclusion includes an unrealistic call to action or weakly appeals to readers to adopt the writer's position.	Conclusion does not include a call to action or an appeal for others to adopt the position.

▶ **Language Conventions**

Standard English spelling, punctuation, capitalization, and manuscript form are used appropriately for this grade level.	Standard English spelling, punctuation, capitalization, and manuscript form are used appropriately for this grade level throughout the editorial.	Standard English spelling, punctuation, capitalization, and manuscript form are used appropriately for this grade level, with few problems.	Inconsistent use of standard English spelling, punctuation, capitalization, and manuscript form disrupts readers' comprehension.	Minimal use of standard English spelling, punctuation, capitalization, and manuscript form confuses readers.
Standard English sentence and paragraph structure, grammar, usage, and diction are used appropriately for this grade level.	Standard English sentence and paragraph structure, grammar, usage, and diction are used appropriately for this grade level throughout the editorial.	Standard English sentence and paragraph structure, grammar, usage, and diction are used appropriately for this grade level, with few problems.	Inconsistent use of standard English sentence and paragraph structure, grammar, usage, and diction disrupts readers' comprehension.	Minimal use of standard English sentence and paragraph structure, grammar, usage, and diction confuses readers.

for **COLLECTION 6** *page 824*   **ANALYTICAL SCALE**

Writing: Analyzing Literature

Use the chart below (and the rubric on page 53) to evaluate a short story analysis. Circle the numbers that best indicate how well the criteria are met. With these nine criteria the lowest possible score is 0, the highest 36.

4 = Clearly meets this criterion

3 = Makes a serious effort to meet this criterion and is fairly successful

2 = Makes some effort to meet this criterion but with little success

1 = Does not achieve this criterion

0 = Unscorable

CRITERIA FOR EVALUATION	RATING
Genre, Organization, and Focus	
Introduction grabs the reader's attention.	4 3 2 1
Introduction identifies the story and its author.	4 3 2 1
Thesis statement identifies the most important literary element and lists the essay's key points.	4 3 2 1
Each body paragraph contains one key point.	4 3 2 1
Key points are supported with evidence from the text.	4 3 2 1
Conclusion restates the thesis and summarizes the key points.	4 3 2 1
Conclusion ends with a comment that connects the analysis to real life.	4 3 2 1
Language Conventions	
Standard English spelling, punctuation, capitalization, and manuscript form are used appropriately for this grade level.	4 3 2 1
Standard English sentence and paragraph structure, grammar, usage, and diction are used appropriately for this grade level.	4 3 2 1
Total Points:	

Writing: Analyzing Literature

CRITERIA FOR EVALUATION	SCORE POINT 4	SCORE POINT 3	SCORE POINT 2	SCORE POINT 1
Genre, Organization, and Focus				
Introduction grabs the reader's attention.	Introduction grabs the reader's attention with an interesting anecdote or by asking questions.	Introduction interests readers but does not grab their attention.	Introduction is only partially successful at engaging the reader's interest.	Introduction lacks an engaging opening and does not interest readers.
Introduction identifies the story and its author.	Introduction clearly identifies the story's title and author.	Essay identifies the story's title and author; however, the introduction does not include this information.	Essay identifies the story's title or author but not both.	Essay does not identify the story's title and author, or the title or author is incorrectly identified.
Thesis statement identifies the most important literary element and lists the essay's key points.	Thesis statement is strong and clear, identifies the literary element to be discussed, and lists all supporting key points.	Thesis statement is weak or unclear, vaguely identifies the literary element to be discussed, or does not list all supporting key points.	Thesis statement is difficult to identify, does not identify the literary element to be discussed, or fails to list any supporting key points.	Thesis statement, the literary element to be discussed, and key points are missing.
Each body paragraph contains one key point.	Each body paragraph focuses attention on only one clear key point and offers appropriate elaboration on that key point.	Each body paragraph contains only one key point. However, the writer does not elaborate sufficiently on several of the essay's key points.	Some body paragraphs contain more than one key point, and elaboration is sometimes missing, confusing, or irrelevant.	Body paragraphs contain more than one key point, or elaboration is often missing.
Key points are supported with evidence from the text.	Writer consistently uses direct textual evidence, including direct quotations, summaries, and paraphrases, to support key points.	Writer usually uses direct textual evidence to support key points, although evidence is sometimes inadequate.	Writer sometimes uses weak or irrelevant evidence to support key points.	Writer often fails to provide evidence to support key points.

CRITERIA FOR EVALUATION	SCORE POINT 4	SCORE POINT 3	SCORE POINT 2	SCORE POINT 1
Conclusion restates the thesis and summarizes the key points.	Conclusion restates the thesis in a new and interesting way and clearly summarizes each key point.	Conclusion restates thesis as it appeared in the introduction or generally identifies the essay's key points.	Conclusion restates thesis in a confusing way or does not identify the essay's key points.	Conclusion omits or incorrectly states the thesis.
Conclusion ends with a comment that connects the analysis to real life.	Conclusion ends with a clearly insightful comment that relates the analysis to life.	Conclusion ends with a bland or cliché statement that relates the analysis to life.	Conclusion includes a confusing or irrelevant statement that loosely connects the analysis to life.	Conclusion does not include a statement that connect the analysis to life.

Language Conventions

CRITERIA FOR EVALUATION	SCORE POINT 4	SCORE POINT 3	SCORE POINT 2	SCORE POINT 1
Standard English spelling, punctuation, capitalization, and manuscript form are used appropriately for this grade level.	Standard English spelling, punctuation, capitalization, and manuscript form are used appropriately for this grade level throughout the essay.	Standard English spelling, punctuation, capitalization, and manuscript form are used appropriately for this grade level, with a few problems.	Inconsistent use of standard English spelling, punctuation, capitalization, and manuscript form disrupts the reader's comprehension.	Minimal use of standard English spelling, punctuation, capitalization, and manuscript form confuses the reader.
Standard English sentence and paragraph structure, grammar, usage, and diction are used appropriately for this grade level.	Standard English sentence and paragraph structure, grammar, usage, and diction are used appropriately for this grade level throughout the essay.	Standard English sentence and paragraph structure, grammar, usage, and diction are used appropriately for this grade level, with a few problems.	Inconsistent use of standard English sentence and paragraph structure, grammar, usage, and diction disrupts the reader's comprehension.	Minimal use of standard English sentence and paragraph structure, grammar, usage, and diction confuses the reader.

      ANALYTICAL SCALE

Speaking: Presenting a Literary Analysis

Use the chart below to evaluate a presentation of a literary analysis. Circle the numbers that best indicate how well the criteria are met. With these seven criteria the lowest possible score is 0, the highest 28.

4 = Clearly meets this criterion

3 = Makes a serious effort to meet this criterion and is fairly successful

2 = Makes some effort to meet this criterion but with little success

1 = Does not achieve this criterion

0 = Unscorable

CRITERIA FOR EVALUATION	RATING
Content, Organization, and Delivery	
Introduction includes clear thesis statement and summary of key points.	4 3 2 1
Speaker supports key points with sufficient evidence.	4 3 2 1
Speaker uses listener-friendly techniques, such as rhetorical questions and parallel structure.	4 3 2 1
Presentation follows chronological order or order of importance.	4 3 2 1
Speaker effectively uses note cards to keep important points in mind.	4 3 2 1
Speaker uses verbal and nonverbal techniques effectively.	4 3 2 1
Language Conventions	
Standard English grammar, usage, and diction are used appropriately for this grade level.	4 3 2 1
Total Points:	

for **COLLECTION 7** *page 1098*

ANALYTICAL SCALE

Writing: Reporting Literary Research

Use the chart below (and the rubric on pages 57–58) to evaluate a literary research paper. Circle the numbers that best indicate how well the criteria are met. With these eleven criteria the lowest possible score is 0, the highest 44.

4 = Clearly meets this criterion

3 = Makes a serious effort to meet this criterion and is fairly successful

2 = Makes some effort to meet this criterion but with little success

1 = Does not achieve this criterion

0 = Unscorable

CRITERIA FOR EVALUATION	RATING
Genre, Organization, and Focus	
Introduction hooks readers with an interesting opening.	4 3 2 1
Introduction provides background information about the author, his or her works, and the period in which he or she wrote.	4 3 2 1
Introduction includes a clear thesis statement.	4 3 2 1
Body paragraphs are organized clearly.	4 3 2 1
Main ideas are supported by facts, details, and examples from research.	4 3 2 1
Sources included in the paper offer different perspectives.	4 3 2 1
Sources are credited and cited correctly.	4 3 2 1
Conclusion restates the thesis in a unique way.	4 3 2 1
Conclusion provides a final insight into the writer's research or the significance of the paper's topic.	4 3 2 1
Language Conventions	
Standard English spelling, punctuation, capitalization, and manuscript form are used appropriately for this grade level.	4 3 2 1
Standard English sentence and paragraph structure, grammar, usage, and diction are used appropriately for this grade level.	4 3 2 1
Total Points:	

for COLLECTION 7 `page 1098`   **ANALYTICAL SCORING RUBRIC**

Writing: Reporting Literary Research

CRITERIA FOR EVALUATION	SCORE POINT 4	SCORE POINT 3	SCORE POINT 2	SCORE POINT 1
Genre, Organization, and Focus				
Introduction hooks readers with an interesting opening.	Introduction successfully hooks the reader's attention with an interesting opening.	Introduction attempts to interest readers but does not grab their attention.	Introduction is only partially successful at engaging the reader's attention.	Introduction lacks an engaging opening.
Introduction provides background information about the author, his or her works, and the period in which he or she wrote.	Introduction provides all relevant background information.	Introduction provides most relevant background information, but some information is incomplete or may be located elsewhere in the paper.	Introduction is missing several important pieces of background information.	Introduction does not provide background information or information is not relevant.
Introduction includes a clear thesis statement.	Introduction includes a strong, focused thesis statement.	Introduction includes an overly general thesis statement.	Introduction includes a weak or confusing thesis statement.	Introduction does not include a thesis statement.
Body paragraphs are organized clearly.	All body paragraphs are ordered clearly and effectively, using one or more organizational patterns.	Most body paragraphs are organized clearly, but the organizational pattern of some paragraphs is unclear.	Body paragraphs are ordered in a confusing or inappropriate way.	Body paragraphs are disordered.
Main ideas are supported by facts, details, and examples from research.	All main ideas are well supported by specific facts, details, and examples from the writer's research.	Most main ideas are supported by facts, details, and examples from the writer's research, although some support is inadequate.	Several main ideas are supported by irrelevant, confusing, or inadequate facts, details, and examples from the writer's research.	Main ideas are not supported by information from the writer's research.
Sources included in the paper offer different perspectives.	Sources, such as magazine articles, Web articles, and books, offer a balanced variety of perspectives.	Paper includes support from a variety of sources, but perspectives are generally the same.	Limited variety of sources include only one or two authors with similar backgrounds and perspectives.	Paper does not include appropriate sources.

CRITERIA FOR EVALUATION	SCORE POINT 4	SCORE POINT 3	SCORE POINT 2	SCORE POINT 1
Sources are credited and cited correctly.	All sources are credited when necessary, and all citations are correctly placed and punctuated.	Most sources are credited when necessary, or some citations are incorrectly placed and punctuated.	Several sources are not credited when necessary, or several citations are incorrectly placed and punctuated.	Most sources are not credited when necessary, or citations are incorrectly placed and punctuated.
Conclusion restates the thesis in a unique way.	Conclusion restates the thesis in a new and interesting way.	Conclusion restates the thesis exactly or almost exactly as it appears in the introduction.	Conclusion states a different thesis, or the thesis is restated in a confusing way.	Conclusion does not restate the thesis.
Conclusion provides a final insight into the writer's research or the significance of the paper's topic.	Conclusion effectively closes by providing a clear, interesting insight into the writer's research or the topic's significance.	Conclusion closes by providing a clear, uninteresting insight into the writer's research or the topic's significance.	Conclusion closes by providing a final, confusing insight into the writer's research or the topic's significance.	Conclusion does not offer a final insight into the writer's research or the topic's significance.

▶ **Language Conventions**

CRITERIA FOR EVALUATION	SCORE POINT 4	SCORE POINT 3	SCORE POINT 2	SCORE POINT 1
Standard English spelling, punctuation, capitalization, and manuscript form are used appropriately for this grade level.	Standard English spelling, punctuation, capitalization, and manuscript form are used appropriately for this grade level throughout the essay.	Standard English spelling, punctuation, capitalization, and manuscript form are used appropriately for this grade level, with a few problems.	Inconsistent use of standard English spelling, punctuation, capitalization, and manuscript form disrupts the reader's comprehension.	Minimal use of standard English spelling, punctuation, capitalization, and manuscript form confuses the reader.
Standard English sentence and paragraph structure, grammar, usage, and diction are used appropriately for this grade level.	Standard English sentence and paragraph structure, grammar, usage, and diction are used appropriately for this grade level.	Standard English sentence and paragraph structure, grammar, usage, and diction are used appropriately for this grade level, with a few problems.	Inconsistent use of standard English sentence and paragraph structure, grammar, usage, and diction disrupts the reader's comprehension.	Minimal use of standard English sentence and paragraph structure, grammar, usage, and diction confuses the reader.

ANALYTICAL SCALE

Speaking: Presenting Literary Research

Use the chart below to evaluate an oral report of literary research. Circle the numbers that best indicate how well the criteria are met. With these nine criteria the lowest possible score is 0, the highest 36.

4 = Clearly meets this criterion

3 = Makes a serious effort to meet this criterion and is fairly successful

2 = Makes some effort to meet this criterion but with little success

1 = Does not achieve this criterion

0 = Unscorable

WORKSHOP SCALES AND RUBRICS

CRITERIA FOR EVALUATION	RATING
Content, Organization, and Delivery	
Lively introduction uses an interesting fact, intriguing quotation, or challenging question to seize the audience's attention.	4 3 2 1
Clear and concise thesis statement is introduced in the opening minutes of the presentation.	4 3 2 1
Speaker uses simplified vocabulary, shorter sentences, and effective transitional expressions to make the presentation easy for listeners to understand.	4 3 2 1
A combination of exposition, narration, and description are effectively used to make the presentation informative and entertaining. Visuals, if used, are relevant and clear.	4 3 2 1
Presentation uses a variety of primary and secondary sources without overloading the audience with bibliographic information, and the speaker identifies sources only for important quotations, facts, or conclusions.	4 3 2 1
Conclusion repeats and emphasizes the presentation's thesis.	4 3 2 1
Speaker uses note cards to deliver presentation extemporaneously.	4 3 2 1
Speaker uses verbal and nonverbal techniques effectively.	4 3 2 1
Language Conventions	
Standard English grammar, usage, and diction are used appropriately for this grade level.	4 3 2 1
Total Points:	

Media: Creating a Multimedia Presentation

Use the chart below to evaluate a multimedia presentation. Circle the numbers that best indicate how well the criteria are met. With these seven criteria the lowest possible score is 0, the highest 28.

4 = Clearly meets this criterion

3 = Makes a serious effort to meet this criterion and is fairly successful

2 = Makes some effort to meet this criterion but with little success

1 = Does not achieve this criterion

0 = Unscorable

CRITERIA FOR EVALUATION	RATING
Content, Organization, and Delivery	
Presentation analyzes one or more works of literature and the culture or country from which the literature is derived.	4 3 2 1
Thesis statement clearly presents the focus of the presentation and encompasses the presenter's ideas.	4 3 2 1
Presentation effectively uses text, images, and sounds to elaborate on spoken content.	4 3 2 1
Presentation uses a wide variety of sources, including both print and electronic sources. Speaker documents all sources as necessary.	4 3 2 1
To deliver the presentation, the speaker uses note cards placed in order of importance.	4 3 2 1
Speaker uses verbal and nonverbal techniques effectively.	4 3 2 1
Language Conventions	
Standard English grammar, usage, and diction are used appropriately for this grade level.	4 3 2 1
Total Points:	

Scales and Sample Papers

Analytical Scale: 6 Traits—Plus 1

IDEAS AND CONTENT

Score 5

The paper is clear, focused, and engaging. Its thoughtful, concrete details capture the reader's attention and flesh out the central theme, main idea, or story line.

- *A score "5" paper has the following characteristics.*

  ✓ The topic is clearly focused and manageable for a paper of its kind; it is not overly broad or scattered.
  ✓ Ideas are original and creative.
  ✓ The writer appears to be working from personal knowledge or experience.
  ✓ Key details are insightful and well considered; they are not obvious, predictable, or humdrum.
  ✓ The development of the topic is thorough and purposeful; the writer anticipates and answers the reader's questions.
  ✓ Supporting details are never superfluous or merely ornamental; every detail contributes to the whole.

Score 3

The writer develops the topic in a general or basic way; although clear, the paper remains routine or broad.

- *A score "3" paper has the following characteristics.*

  ✓ Although the topic may be fuzzy, it is still possible to understand the writer's purpose and to predict how the paper will be developed.
  ✓ Support is present, but somewhat vague and unhelpful in illustrating the key issues or main idea; the writer makes references to his or her own experience or knowledge, but has difficulty moving from general observations to specifics.
  ✓ Ideas are understandable, yet not detailed, elaborated upon, or personalized; the writer's ideas do not reveal any deep comprehension of the topic or of the writing task.
  ✓ The writer does not stray from the topic, but ideas remain general or slightly implicit; more information is necessary to fill in the gaps.

Score 1

The paper does not exhibit any clear purpose or main idea. The reader must use the scattered details to infer a coherent and meaningful message.

- *A score "1" paper has the following characteristics.*

  ✓ The writer seems not to have truly settled on a topic; the essay reads like a series of brainstorming notes or disconnected, random thoughts.
  ✓ The thesis is a vague statement of the topic rather than a main idea about the topic; in addition, there is little or no support or detail.
  ✓ Information is very limited or vague; readers must make inferences to fill in gaps of logic or to identify any progression of ideas.
  ✓ Text may be rambling and repetitious; alternatively, the length may not be adequate for a thoughtful development of ideas.
  ✓ There is no subordination of ideas; every idea seems equally weighted or ideas are not tied to an overarching idea.

ORGANIZATION

Score 5

Organization enables the clear communication of the central idea or story line. The order of information draws the reader effortlessly through the text.

- *A score "5" paper has the following characteristics.*

  ✓ The sequencing is logical and effective; ideas and details "fit" where the writer has placed them.

  ✓ The essay contains an interesting or inviting introduction and a satisfying conclusion.

  ✓ The pacing is carefully controlled; the writer slows down to provide explanation or elaboration when appropriate and increases the pace when necessary.

  ✓ Transitions carefully connect ideas and cue the reader to specific relationships between ideas.

  ✓ The choice of organizational structure is appropriate to the writer's purpose and audience.

  ✓ If present, the title sums up the central idea of the paper in a fresh or thoughtful way.

Score 3

Organization is reasonably strong; it enables the reader to move continually forward without undue confusion.

- *A score "3" paper has the following characteristics.*

  ✓ The essay has an introduction and conclusion. However, the introduction may not be inviting or engaging; the conclusion may not knit all the paper's ideas together with a summary or restatement.

  ✓ Sequencing is logical but predictable. Sometimes, the sequence may be so formulaic that it detracts from the content.

  ✓ At times, the sequence may not consistently support the essay's ideas; the reader may wish to reorder sections mentally or to supply transitions as he or she reads.

  ✓ Pacing is reasonably well done, although sometimes the writer moves ahead too quickly or spends too much time on unimportant details.

  ✓ At times, transitions may be fuzzy, showing unclear connections between ideas.

  ✓ If present, the title may be dull or a simple restatement of the topic or prompt.

Score 1

Writing does not exhibit a sense of purpose or writing strategy. Ideas, details, or events appear to be cobbled together without any internal structure.

- *A score "1" paper has the following characteristics.*

  ✓ Sequencing needs work; one idea or event does not logically follow another. Organizational problems make it difficult for the reader to understand the main idea.

  ✓ There is no real introduction to guide the reader into the paper; neither is there any real conclusion or attempt to tie things up at the end.

  ✓ Pacing is halting or inconsistent; the writer may slow the pace or speed up at inappropriate times.

  ✓ Ideas are connected with confusing transitions; alternatively, connections are altogether absent.

  ✓ If present, the title does not accurately reflect the content of the essay.

Analytical Scale: 6 Traits—Plus 1 *(continued)*

VOICE

Score 5

The writing is expressive and engaging. In addition, the writer seems to have a clear awareness of audience and purpose.

- *A score "5" paper has the following characteristics.*

  ✓ The tone of the writing is appropriate for the purpose and audience of the paper.

  ✓ The reader is aware of a real person behind the text; if appropriate, the writer takes risks in revealing a personal dimension throughout the piece.

  ✓ If the paper is expository or persuasive, the writer shows a strong connection to the topic and explains why the reader should care about the issue.

  ✓ If the paper is a narrative, the point of view is sincere, interesting, and compelling.

Score 3

The writer is reasonably genuine but does not reveal any excitement or connection with the issue. The resulting paper is pleasant but not truly engaging.

- *A score "3" paper has the following characteristics.*

  ✓ The writer offers obvious generalities instead of personal insights.

  ✓ The writer uses neutral language and a slightly flattened tone.

  ✓ The writer communicates in an earnest and pleasing manner, yet takes no risks. In only a few instances is the reader captivated or moved.

  ✓ Expository or persuasive writing does not reveal a consistent engagement with the topic; there is no attempt to build credibility with the audience.

  ✓ Narrative writing doesn't reveal a fresh or individual perspective.

Score 1

Writing is mechanical or wooden. The writer appears indifferent to the topic and/or the audience.

- *A score "1" paper has the following characteristics.*

  ✓ The writer shows no concern with the audience; the voice may be jarringly inappropriate for the intended reader.

  ✓ The development of the topic is so limited that no identifiable point of view is present; or the writing is so short that it offers little but a general introduction of the topic.

  ✓ The writer seems to speak in a monotone, using a voice that suppresses all excitement about the message.

  ✓ Although the writing may communicate on a functional level, the writing is ordinary and takes no risks; depending on the topic, it may be overly technical or jargonistic.

WORD CHOICE

Score 5

Words are precise, engaging, and unaffected. They convey the writer's message in an interesting and effective way.

- *A score "5" paper has the following characteristics.*

  ✓ All words are specific and appropriate. In all instances, the writer has taken care to choose the right words or phrases.
  ✓ The paper's language is natural, not overwrought; it never shows a lack of control. Clichés and jargon are rarely used.
  ✓ The paper contains energetic verbs; precise nouns and modifiers provide clarity.
  ✓ The writer uses vivid words and phrases, including sensory details; such language creates distinct images in the reader's mind.

Score 3

Despite its lack of flair, the paper's language gets the message across. It is functional and clear.

- *A score "3" paper has the following characteristics.*

  ✓ Words are correct and generally adequate, but lack originality or precision.
  ✓ Familiar words and phrases do not pique the reader's interest or imagination. Lively verbs and phrases perk things up occasionally, but the paper does not consistently sparkle.
  ✓ There are attempts at engaging or academic language, but they sometimes seem overly showy or pretentious.
  ✓ The writing contains passive verbs and basic nouns and adjectives, and it lacks precise adverbs.

Score 1

The writer's limited vocabulary impedes communication; he or she seems to struggle for words to convey a clear message.

- *A score "1" paper has the following characteristics.*

  ✓ Vague language communicates an imprecise or incomplete message. The reader is left confused or unsure of the writer's purpose.
  ✓ Words are used incorrectly. In addition, frequent misuse of parts of speech impairs understanding.
  ✓ Excessive redundancy in the paper is distracting.
  ✓ The writing overuses jargon or clichés.

Analytical Scale: 6 Traits—Plus 1 *(continued)*

SENTENCE FLUENCY

Score 5

Sentences are thoughtfully constructed, and sentence structure is varied throughout the paper. When read aloud, the writing is fluent and rhythmic.

■ *A score "5" paper has the following characteristics.*

✓ The sentences are constructed so that meaning is clear to the reader.

✓ Sentences vary in length and in structure.

✓ Varied sentence beginnings add interest and clarity.

✓ The writing has a steady beat; the reader is able to read the text effortlessly, without confusion or stumbling.

✓ Dialogue, if used, is natural. Any fragments are used purposefully and contribute to the paper's style.

✓ Thoughtful connectives and transitions between sentences reveal how the paper's ideas work together.

Score 3

The text maintains a steady rhythm, but the reader may find it more flat or mechanical than fluent or musical.

■ *A score "3" paper has the following characteristics.*

✓ Sentences are usually grammatical and unified, but they are routine rather than artful. The writer has not paid a great deal of attention to how the sentences sound.

✓ There is some variation in sentence length and structure as well as in sentence beginnings. Not all sentences are constructed exactly the same way.

✓ The reader may have to search for transitional words and phrases that show how sentences relate to one another. Sometimes, such context clues are entirely absent when they should be present.

✓ Although sections of the paper invite expressive oral reading, the reader may also encounter many stilted or awkward sections.

Score 1

The reader will encounter challenges in reading the choppy or confusing text; meaning may be significantly obscured by the errors in sentence construction.

■ *A score "1" paper has the following characteristics.*

✓ The sentences do not "hang together." They are run-on, incomplete, monotonous, or awkward.

✓ Phrasing often sounds too sing-song, not natural. The paper does not invite expressive oral reading.

✓ Nearly all the sentences begin the same way, and they may all follow the same pattern (e.g., subject-verb-object). The result may be a monotonous repetition of sounds.

✓ Endless connectives or a complete lack of connectives creates a confused muddle of language.

CONVENTIONS

Score 5

Standard writing conventions (e.g., spelling, punctuation, capitalization, grammar, usage, and paragraphing) are used correctly and in a way that aids the reader's understanding. Any errors tend to be minor; the piece is nearly ready for publication.

- *A score "5" paper has the following characteristics.*

  ✓ Paragraphing is regular and enhances the organization of the paper.

  ✓ Grammar and usage are correct and add clarity to the text as a whole. Sometimes, the writer may manipulate conventions in a controlled way—especially grammar and spelling—for stylistic effect.

  ✓ Punctuation is accurate; it enables the reader to move through the text with understanding and ease.

  ✓ The writer's understanding of capitalization rules is evident throughout the paper.

  ✓ Most words, even difficult ones, are spelled correctly.

Score 3

The writer exhibits an awareness of a limited set of standard writing conventions and uses them to enhance the paper's readability. Although the writer shows control, at times errors distract the reader or impede communication. Moderate editing is required for publication.

- *A score "3" paper has the following characteristics.*

  ✓ Paragraphs are used, but may begin in the wrong places, or sections that should be separate paragraphs are run together.

  ✓ Conventions may not always be correct. However, problems with grammar and usage are usually not serious enough to distort meaning.

  ✓ Terminal (end-of-sentence) punctuation is usually correct; internal punctuation (e.g., commas, apostrophes, semicolons, parentheses) may be missing or wrong.

  ✓ Common words are usually spelled correctly.

  ✓ Most words are capitalized correctly, but the writer's command of more sophisticated capitalization skills is inconsistent.

Score 1

There are errors in spelling, punctuation, grammar and usage, capitalization, and/or paragraphing that seriously impede the reader's comprehension. Extensive editing is required for publication.

- *A score "1" paper has the following characteristics.*

  ✓ Paragraphing is missing, uneven, or too frequent. Most of the paragraphs do not reinforce or support the organizational structure of the paper.

  ✓ Errors in grammar and usage are very common and distracting; such errors also affect the paper's meaning.

  ✓ Punctuation, including terminal punctuation, is often missing or incorrect.

  ✓ Even common words are frequently misspelled.

  ✓ Capitalization is haphazard or reveals the writer's understanding of only the simplest rules.

  ✓ The paper must be read once just to decode the language and then again to capture the paper's meaning.

Analytical Scale: 6 Traits—Plus 1 *(continued)*

PRESENTATION

Score 5

The presentation of the writing is clear and visually appealing. The format helps the reader focus on the message of the writing.

- *A score "5" paper has the following characteristics.*
  - ✓ If the paper is handwritten, all letters are formed clearly, and the slant and spacing are consistent.
  - ✓ If the paper is word processed, fonts and font sizes are appropriate for the genre of writing and assist the reader's comprehension.
  - ✓ White space and text are balanced.
  - ✓ Text markers, such as title, headings, and numbering, highlight important information and aid reading of the text.
  - ✓ If visuals are used, they are appropriate to the writing, are integrated effectively with the text, and clearly communicate and enhance the message.

Score 3

The presentation of the writing is readable and understandable; however, inconsistencies in format at times detract from the text.

- *A score "3" paper has the following characteristics.*
  - ✓ If the paper is handwritten, the handwriting is legible, but some inconsistencies occur in spacing and the formation and slant of letters.
  - ✓ If the paper is word processed, fonts and font sizes are inconsistent, sometimes distracting the reader.
  - ✓ White space and text are consistent, although a different use of space would make the paper easier to read.
  - ✓ Text markers, such as title, headings, and numbering, are used to some degree; however, they are inconsistent and only occasionally helpful to the reader.
  - ✓ Visuals are sometimes ineffective and not clearly linked to the text.

Score 1

The presentation and format of the writing are confusing, making the paper difficult to read and understand.

- *A score "1" paper has the following characteristics.*
  - ✓ If the paper is handwritten, the letters are formed incorrectly or irregularly. The inconsistent slant and spacing make the paper difficult to read.
  - ✓ If the paper is word processed, fonts and font sizes are used randomly or inappropriately, disrupting the reader's comprehension.
  - ✓ Spacing appears random, with use of white space either excessive or minimal.
  - ✓ Text markers, such as title, headings, and numbering, are not used.
  - ✓ Visuals are inaccurate, inappropriate, misleading, or confusing.

Holistic Scale
Biographical or Autobiographical Narrative

<table>
<tr><td>

Score 4

This distinctly purposeful narrative has an engaging and meaningful introduction, presents a logical sequence of events, and relies on concrete sensory details. The significance of the events is clearly communicated.

</td><td>

■ *The writing strongly demonstrates*

✓ thorough attention to all parts of the writing task

✓ a strong and meaningful purpose, consistent tone and focus, and thoughtfully effective organization

✓ a distinct understanding of audience

✓ great proficiency in relating a sequence of events and their significance to the audience

✓ consistent use of concrete sensory details to describe the sights, sounds, and smells of a scene

✓ variation of sentence types using precise, descriptive language

✓ a solid command of English-language conventions. Errors, if any, are minor and unobtrusive.

</td></tr>
<tr><td>

Score 3

This purposeful narrative has a meaningful introduction, presents a logical sequence of events, and clearly communicates the significance of those events.

</td><td>

■ *The writing generally demonstrates*

✓ attention to all parts of the writing task

✓ clear purpose, a consistent tone and focus, and effective organization

✓ an understanding of audience

✓ an ability to relate a sequence of events and their significance to the audience

✓ frequent use of concrete sensory details to describe the sights, sounds, and smells of a scene

✓ variation of sentence types using some descriptive language

✓ a command of English-language conventions. Few errors exist, and they do not interfere with the reader's understanding of the narrative.

</td></tr>
<tr><td>

Score 2

This narrative has a somewhat vague introduction. The sequence or significance of the events is unclear.

</td><td>

■ *The writing demonstrates*

✓ attention to only parts of the writing task

✓ vague purpose, an inconsistent tone and focus, and less than effective organization

✓ little or no understanding of audience

✓ a weak ability to relate a sequence of events and their significance to the audience

✓ infrequent use of concrete sensory details to describe the sights, sounds, and smells of a scene

✓ little variation in sentence type; use of basic, predictable descriptive language

✓ inconsistent use of English-language conventions. Errors may interfere with the reader's understanding of the narrative.

</td></tr>
</table>

Score 1

This narrative has a vague introduction and displays no clear purpose. Events are disorganized and their significance is hidden.

■ *The writing lacks*

✓ attention to most parts of the writing task

✓ a purpose (or provides only a weak sense of purpose), a focus, and effective organization

✓ an understanding of audience

✓ proficiency in relating a sequence of events to the audience

✓ concrete sensory details to describe the sights, sounds, and smells of a scene

✓ sentence variety and descriptive vocabulary

✓ a basic understanding of English-language conventions. Numerous errors often interfere with the reader's understanding of the narrative.

Sample A: Autobiographical Narrative

> **PROMPT**
>
> Can you think of an experience that has changed the way you think about something? Write an autobiographical narrative about an experience that has had a significant effect on you, relating the events and their significance. Remember to use narrative and descriptive details to describe the events.

When I started eighth grade at a new school, I was worried about the change. I wanted people to think that I was cool, so I knew I had to be careful when choosing my new friends.

Because I was temporarily friendless, I was able to focus on my studies. I scored well on papers, and my classmates began coming to me for help.

One day I felt a tap on my shoulder from Kenneth, the guy who sat behind me. "Hey Sue, will you read my essay?" he whispered. Kenneth was a misfit, and he always mumbled. I was embarrassed that he had spoken to me, and a couple of classmates made "kissy" faces. Still, I ignored them and read Kenneth's essay. It was full of mistakes. I quickly marked up the essay and handed it back.

From then on, every week Kenneth asked me to read his assignment. I clucked over his typos and praised him when he wrote something well. And certainly his compliments of "Sue, you're so smart" fed my ego!

Then our little situation blew up. The assignment was to write a poem. I felt the familiar tap on my shoulder as we sat waiting for Mr. Brockett to begin class. I secretly reached back to take Kenneth's poem but felt nothing but air. I looked around and saw Mr. Brockett holding the paper. He said sternly to Kenneth, "Why are you passing notes?"

Kenneth stammered, "It's not a . . . not a—" but Mr. Brockett interrupted. "I think Kenneth should share his note, shouldn't he?" Students around us said, "Yeah!" and clapped. "Come read your note, Kenneth," Mr. Brockett said.

Kenneth looked upset. He walked slowly to the front and stared at his paper. He began reading quietly. "She's lovely and fair, and always there." Mr. Brockett

Sample A: Autobiographical Narrative (continued)

interrupted him. "Okay, Kenneth." Then he glanced at the poem, whispered something, and sent Kenneth back to his desk. Mr. Brockett handed the poem to me. I was surprised, but I read the rest of it. It was a love poem.

I wasn't sure how to respond. Mortified, I turned to glare at Kenneth, who was bent over his desk. When he glanced up at me, I turned away. Then Mr. Brockett coughed and started class again.

As soon as the bell rang, I left the room without saying a word to Kenneth. I felt utterly embarrassed.

The next day, Kenneth wasn't in class. I went up to Mr. Brockett and asked whether Kenneth was sick, but Mr. Brockett shook his head. "I think you should talk to him, Sue. You were probably one of his closest friends."

I looked at Mr. Brockett silently. His guilt trip sure was working! But I knew he was right. I felt ashamed that I hadn't even looked at Kenneth as I headed out of class.

One thing was clear. Kenneth needed a good friend, and I knew how that felt. That night I called him. After a deep breath I said, "I'm sorry I didn't say anything. Your poem just surprised me." After a moment of silence, Kenneth said haltingly, "There is that research paper coming up. Think you could help with that?"

I breathed a sigh of relief. "All right," I laughed. "Just make sure it's not about love poetry. Okay?"

Sample A Evaluation: Autobiographical Narrative

Holistic Scale

Rating: 4 points

Note: This essay illustrates the type of development appropriate for the prompt, but some teachers may ask their students for longer essays.

Comments: This is a thoughtful autobiographical narrative that shows a thorough understanding of all aspects of the writing task. The narrative is well organized and purposeful, with concrete sensory details describing the sequence of events. The significance of the events is clearly communicated. Tone and focus are consistent and appropriate. Sentences are varied and clear in meaning. The narrative shows a solid command of English-language conventions.

Analytical Scale: 6 Traits—Plus 1

Ratings (High score is 5.)

Ideas and Content: 4	**Sentence Fluency: 4**
Organization: 4	**Conventions: 5**
Voice: 5	**Presentation: 4**
Word Choice: 4	

Comments:

Ideas and Content: A personal experience at school is used to relate an interesting sequence of events that significantly affected the writer's relationship to a friend.

Organization: Dialogue helps grab the reader's interest. The sequence of events is presented clearly and logically.

Voice: The tone is appropriate for an autobiographical narrative. A personal dimension is revealed throughout the essay, and the point of view is sincere and compelling.

Word Choice: The narrative's language is natural. Words are specific and appropriate.

Sentence Fluency: Sentences are clear in meaning and are often varied in length and structure, although they are occasionally choppy. Transitions usually help the reader understand relationships between ideas. Dialogue is natural and purposeful.

Conventions: Effective paragraphing enhances the essay's organization, and the writer demonstrates a strong command of English-language conventions.

Presentation: The presentation is simple and clear.

Sample B: Autobiographical Narrative

PROMPT

Can you think of an experience that has changed the way you think about something? Write an autobiographical narrative about an experience that has had a significant effect on you, relating the events and their significance. Remember to use narrative and descriptive details to describe the events.

I was starting eighth grade at a new school and wanted to be part of the cool crowd. After a month, I started acing tests. Other kids started coming to me for help. I was happy to help. It was a good way to make friends.

This guy Kenneth was kind of a loser. He mumbled all the time, and he wore wrinkled shirts. One day he asked me for help, so I helped him.

From then on, Kenneth kept asking me to help. I enjoyed feeling like Kenneth's teacher. He'd say things like "Sue, you're so smart!" That was sort of cool.

One day our asignment was to write a poem. Kenneth asked me to read his. I tried to but Mr. Brockett grabbed the poem. He asked why Kenneth was passing notes and asked the class, "Would everyone like to hear Kenneth's note?"

Kenneth started reading his poem, but Mr. Brockett stopped him and handed the poem to me. It was a love poem.

Kenneth had the wrong idea! I left without saying a word to him. The next day Kenneth wasn't in class. I asked Mr. Brockett whether Kenneth was sick. Mr. Brockett said, "Kenneth got confused. And you were maybe his only friend here."

What a guilt trip! But I knew he was right. Kenneth was really hurting, not me.

That night I called Kenneth. I told him I was sorry but I was suprised by what he wrote. Kenneth said, "Can you help me with the research paper?"

I said, "Just don't write any more poems!"

Sample B Evaluation: Autobiographical Narrative

Holistic Scale

Rating: 3 points

Comments: This autobiographical narrative shows a general understanding of the writing task. The narrative is logically organized, and the significance of the events is communicated. Focus is consistent; however, an informal tone detracts from the essay's effectiveness, and parts of the essay need greater development. Sentences are varied and clear in meaning. The narrative shows an adequate understanding of English-language conventions.

Analytical Scale: 6 Traits—Plus 1

Ratings (High score is 5.)

Ideas and Content: 2	**Sentence Fluency: 3**
Organization: 3	**Conventions: 3**
Voice: 2	**Presentation: 4**
Word Choice: 3	

Comments:

Ideas and Content: A personal experience at school is used to relate a sequence of events that significantly affected the writer's relationship with another student. However, the narrative lacks the details necessary to support the main idea fully.

Organization: Sentences and paragraphs flow somewhat smoothly, although effective transitions are sometimes lacking.

Voice: The tone is common to autobiographical narratives, although it is overly informal. A personal dimension is revealed, but too few concrete sensory details are provided.

Word Choice: The narrative's language is natural; however, word choices are often excessively informal. Some words and phrases, such as *acing, loser,* and *guilt trip,* are inappropriate.

Sentence Fluency: Sentences are clear in meaning and vary in structure, but they lack flair. A lack of transitions between ideas confuses the reader. Dialogue is natural, although the adult's speech seems too juvenile.

Conventions: The narrative shows an adequate understanding of English-language conventions but contains several spelling and punctuation errors.

Presentation: The presentation is simple and clear.

Sample C: Autobiographical Narrative

PROMPT

Can you think of an experience that has changed the way you think about something? Write an autobiographical narrative about an experience that has had a significant effect on you, relating the events and their significance. Remember to use narrative and descriptive details to describe the events.

Have you ever been so embarassed you could hardly breath? Well I have. In eighth grade this one guy Kenneth I knew was kind of a looser. I never could understand anythig he said and his clothes were lame. So one day he asks me for help. People were making fun of us, but I read his essay anyway. Wow it was bad so I had to fix it.

Everyday Kenneth kept asking me to read his homework. I started liking feeling like a teacher. He was always saying "Sue, your smart!" One day we wrote poems. He asked me to read his. I tried to but Mr. Brockett grabbed the paper. He thought Kenneth was passing notes. Mr. Brockett told Kenneth to go up front and read his note to the class.

Kenneth was freaking out but he walked up front. He starts reading the poem but Mr Brockett stops him. It was about me! Luckily I was the only one who knew it. After the bell rang, I took off and didn't even look at Kenneth. The next two days he wasn't around so I went to Mr. Brockett and asked if Kenneth was sick? Mr. Brockett said I should talk to him.

Mr. Brockett was like, Kenneth got confused. You were maybe his best friend."

He was right. Since I didn't say anything, Kenneth was probably more upset than me.

I called Kenneth. I told him I was sorry and not to write anymore poems! He was OK with that.

Sample C Evaluation: Autobiographical Narrative

Holistic Scale

Rating: 2 points

Comments: This autobiographical narrative shows a limited understanding of the writing task. The narrative is logically organized, but the significance of the events is vague. The tone is overly informal, although generally consistent, and the topic is unfocused and poorly developed. Sentences are clear in meaning but lack variety in length and structure. The narrative shows a poor understanding of English-language conventions.

Analytical Scale: 6 Traits—Plus 1

Ratings (High score is 5.)

Ideas and Content: 2	**Sentence Fluency: 2**
Organization: 2	**Conventions: 1**
Voice: 2	**Presentation: 3**
Word Choice: 2	

Comments:

Ideas and Content: The main idea is extremely vague, leaving the reader to make inferences to fill in gaps. The narrative lacks development, and the ending is anticlimactic.

Organization: Sentences and paragraphs are in a logical order but do not flow smoothly. Paragraph breaks are not used in appropriate places. Many transitions are lacking.

Voice: The tone is generally sincere, but it is overly informal. A limited personal dimension is demonstrated, but the writer takes few risks.

Word Choice: The narrative's language is natural; however, words are general and basic rather than specific. Words and phrases such as *lame, freaking out,* and *took off* are inappropriate.

Sentence Fluency: Sentences are generally clear in meaning, but they lack variety in length and structure. The narrative lacks adequate transitions and is occasionally muddled.

Conventions: The narrative shows a poor understanding of English-language conventions. Multiple errors exist in grammar, spelling, and punctuation.

Presentation: The presentation is simple and clear.

Holistic Scale
Exposition

Score 4 This expository writing presents a clear thesis or controlling impression and supports it with precise, relevant evidence.	■ *The writing strongly demonstrates* ✓ a clear understanding of all parts of the writing task ✓ a meaningful thesis or controlling impression, a consistent tone and focus, and a purposeful control of organization ✓ use of specific details and examples to support the main ideas ✓ a variety of sentence types using precise, descriptive language ✓ a clear understanding of audience ✓ inclusion of accurate information from all relevant perspectives ✓ anticipation of and thorough attention to readers' possible misunderstandings, biases, and expectations ✓ a solid command of English-language conventions. Errors, if any, are generally minor and unobtrusive.
Score 3 This expository writing presents a thesis or controlling impression and supports it with evidence.	■ *The writing generally demonstrates* ✓ an understanding of all parts of the writing task ✓ a thesis or controlling impression, a consistent tone and focus, and a control of organization ✓ use of details and examples to support the main ideas ✓ a variety of sentence types using some descriptive language ✓ an understanding of audience ✓ inclusion of accurate information from relevant perspectives ✓ anticipation of and attention to readers' possible misunderstandings, biases, and expectations ✓ an understanding of English-language conventions. Some errors exist, but they do not interfere with the reader's understanding.
Score 2 This expository writing presents a thesis or controlling impression, but the thesis is not sufficiently supported.	■ *The writing demonstrates* ✓ an understanding of only parts of the writing task ✓ a thesis or controlling impression (though not always); an inconsistent tone and focus; and little, if any, control of organization ✓ use of limited, if any, details and examples to support the main ideas ✓ little variation in sentence types; use of basic, predictable language ✓ little or no understanding of audience ✓ little or no inclusion of information from relevant perspectives

Holistic Scale
Exposition *(continued)*

✓ little, if any, anticipation of and attention to readers'
possible misunderstandings, biases, and expectations

✓ inconsistent use of English-language conventions.
Several errors exist and may interfere with the reader's
understanding.

■ *The writing lacks*

✓ an understanding of the writing task, addressing only
one part

✓ a thesis or controlling impression (or provides only a
weak one), a focus, and control of organization

✓ details and examples to support ideas

✓ sentence variety and adequate vocabulary

✓ an understanding of audience

✓ accurate information from relevant perspectives

✓ anticipation of and attention to readers' possible
misunderstandings, biases, and expectations

✓ an understanding of English-language conventions.
(Serious errors interfere with the reader's understanding.)

Sample A: Exposition

> **PROMPT**
>
> Is there anything about your high school you wish you could change? Think of an issue in your school that you feel strongly about. Write an editorial for your school newspaper about a situation you wish you could change. Remember to include reasons and relevant evidence to develop a sustained argument.

A few days ago, I had to stand in line in the cafeteria nearly twenty minutes before I got my food during my precious lunch break. Then, I couldn't find a place to sit. The cafeteria was teeming with students cramming down their lunches. I had to smuggle my food into the library and hope the school librarian didn't throw me out for eating my bean burrito next to the encyclopedias. It was a very stressful lunch. And the cause of all this? We have a closed campus for all four grades, which forces our high school to pack students into a too-small cafeteria. The simplest remedy for this problem would be to allow seniors the opportunity to leave campus for lunch.

The issue of an open lunch has come up before. In the past, administrators were worried about students speeding back and forth to restaurants during a forty-five-minute break. Teachers didn't want to deal with tardy students who got caught in traffic and missed the bell.

The first claim sounds valid. But why is it acceptable for students to drive to and from school at the beginning and end of the school day but not at lunchtime? The only difference is the limited amount of time for lunch. If we added ten minutes to the lunchtime break, we might be able to avoid having students speeding back to school. It is certainly worth lengthening the school day by ten minutes if it means students don't have to stand in the cafeteria line for twenty minutes.

As for the concern over tardy students, we could implement a policy of excluding those students who are tardy from the open-lunch benefit. Basically, if students were tardy even one time, they'd lose their privilege of leaving the campus at lunchtime.

Sample A: Exposition *(continued)*

Administrators and teachers could also use open lunch as an incentive for academic achievement and good classroom behavior. Seniors who are failing their classes and/or misbehaving in class would not be allowed to leave campus at lunchtime. The threat of losing open-lunch privileges might be a powerful deterrent for many students.

High school seniors are just a year from entering the "real world," whether it be attending universities or beginning careers. This means that we need to learn and accept adult responsibilities. Open lunches ask seniors to be more responsible, but how can we learn to be responsible without a chance to show administrators and teachers? After all, the government trusts us at sixteen years old to drive 2,000-pound automobiles. Why shouldn't we be trusted to leave school campus during lunch? Let's at least have a trial run with open lunches and see what happens. It might be a win-win situation for everyone, including the school librarian!

Sample A Evaluation: Exposition

Holistic Scale

Rating: 4 points

Note: This essay illustrates the type of development appropriate for the prompt, but some teachers may ask their students for longer essays.

Comments: This essay shows that the writer has a clear understanding of all parts of the writing task. The introduction presents a clear position that is well supported by the body's reasons and evidence. The tone is appropriate, and the paper is logically organized. The writer presents the problem of a crowded lunchroom using personal evidence. Possible counterarguments are addressed by presenting a deterrent to poor academic performance and classroom behavior—the loss of open-lunch privileges. Precise, descriptive language is used, and sentences are varied in length and structure. The writing shows a strong command of English-language conventions.

Analytical Scale: 6 Traits—Plus 1

Ratings (High score is 5.)

Ideas and Content: 5	**Sentence Fluency: 5**
Organization: 5	**Conventions: 4**
Voice: 4	**Presentation: 4**
Word Choice: 4	

Comments:

Ideas and Content: The topic is clearly focused and manageable. Details are insightful and well considered. The writer uses personal knowledge and experience to enhance the writing.

Organization: Ideas are presented in a logical and effective order. The essay includes a clear introduction and conclusion. Transitions help connect ideas and cue the reader to relationships between them.

Voice: The tone is appropriate although slightly informal. The writer reveals a personal dimension by presenting evidence of her own experience with cafeteria overcrowding.

Word Choice: The writing shows careful attention to word choice. Words are specific and appropriate. The language is natural, although a cliché, *win-win situation*, slightly detracts from the essay's message.

Sentence Fluency: A variety of sentence types makes the writing easy to read.

Conventions: The writing demonstrates a strong command of English-language conventions.

Presentation: The presentation is simple and clear.

STUDENT MODEL

Sample B: Exposition

PROMPT

Is there anything about your high school you wish you could change? Think of an issue in your school that you feel strongly about. Write an editorial for your school newspaper about a situation you wish you could change. Remember to include reasons and relevant evidence to develop a sustained argument.

The school cafetaria is too crowded for all of us. People have to stand in line too long, and then the whole lunch period is gone. And we sometimes have nowhere to sit, so we have to go to other rooms to find a place to eat. If we had an open lunch then the cafeteria wouldn't be so crowded for everyone else.

Administrators are worried about students speeding back and forth to restaurants during lunch. Teachers get upset when students are late to class because they took too long at lunch. Maybe if lunch was longer, students wouldn't have to speed back to class. That way we don't have to stand in the cafeteria line for twenty minutes.

As for tardiness, the principle could tell students who are tardy that they don't get to leave school for lunch anymore. If students were tardy even one time, they'd have to eat in the cafetaria everyday for the rest of the year.

The principle and teachers could also use open lunch as a reason for students to get good grades and behave. Senors who aren't doing these things wouldn't be allowed open lunch. If they think they'll lose open lunch, then maybe they'll be good students and not goof off in class.

High school seniors are about to enter the "real world." Why shouldn't they be able to deal with leaving campus for lunch. Open lunches ask seniors to be more responsible, like if we can drive cars at sixteen years old we can leave school for lunch. We should have a practice open lunch. See what happens. The other classes will be stoked because then the cafetaria won't be crowded!

Sample B Evaluation: Exposition

Holistic Scale

Rating: 3 points

Comments: This editorial shows that the writer has a general understanding of all parts of the writing task. The essay presents a clear position that is supported by reasons and evidence, although additional evidence is needed. The tone is generally appropriate; however, some language is too colloquial. The paper is logically organized. Possible counter-arguments are addressed by presenting a deterrent to poor academic performance and classroom behavior—the loss of open-lunch privileges. Sentences are clear in meaning but somewhat monotonous. The writing shows an understanding of English-language conventions, but the essay contains errors in punctuation and spelling.

Analytical Scale: 6 Traits—Plus 1

Ratings (High score is 5.)

Ideas and Content: 4	**Sentence Fluency: 3**
Organization: 3	**Conventions: 2**
Voice: 3	**Presentation: 4**
Word Choice: 2	

Comments:

Ideas and Content: The topic is clearly focused and manageable. However, the essay lacks sufficient specific details and evidence to support the main points fully.

Organization: Ideas are presented in a logical and effective order. The essay includes a clear, although less than engaging, introduction and conclusion. Use of transitions to help connect ideas is adequate.

Voice: The tone is appropriate, although slightly detached. The writer reveals a personal dimension by indicating some experience with cafeteria overcrowding; however, generalities abound.

Word Choice: Words are generally adequate and correct, but they lack originality and precision. Use of slang words, such as *like* and *stoked*, detract from the essay's effectiveness.

Sentence Fluency: Sentences are clear in meaning but are routine rather than creative. Some sentences are repetitive.

Conventions: The writing demonstrates a general understanding of English-language conventions. Errors exist in spelling, punctuation, and grammar.

Presentation: The presentation is simple and clear.

Sample C: Exposition

> **PROMPT**
>
> Is there anything about your high school you wish you could change? Think of an issue in your school that you feel strongly about. Write an editorial for your school newspaper about a situation you wish you could change. Remember to include reasons and relevant evidence to develop a sustained argument.

The school cafetaria is too crowded! I wanted to get a burito yesterday and I was in line too long. I didn't have anywhere to sit because the football and basketball teams had taken up the middle of the cafetaria, and all the band kids were in the back. I thought I saw a seat next to the science brainiacs but than someone's laptop was in that seat and they wouldn't move it. I mumbled, "I don't have time for this stupid stuff, but whatever." Then I snuck into the library and hid my bean burito from Mr. Martin.

I wish I could head down the street to Burito Barn but we aren't allowed to. Why is that! I guess the principle thinks we're going to speed and get tickets from the police. And then we'll be late to class which will make the teachers mad. But we need to have open lunch at this school, the cafetaria is packed to the gills with students! The principle and teachers could tell students they couldn't have open lunch if they were failing all there classes or misbehaving somehow. High school seniors are about to enter the real world. We should be able to leave school at lunchtime. Here we drive cars to school, but we cant even have lunch down the street!

Sample C Evaluation: Exposition

Holistic Scale

Rating: 2 points

Comments: This editorial is poorly developed and shows that the writer does not understand all parts of the writing task. The position is not presented in the introduction; instead, it appears in the concluding paragraph. Possible counterarguments are addressed by presenting a deterrent to poor academic performance and classroom behavior—the loss of open-lunch privileges. Sentences are clear in meaning but somewhat monotonous. The writing shows a poor understanding of English-language conventions; the essay contains many errors in punctuation, grammar, and spelling.

Analytical Scale: 6 Traits—Plus 1

Ratings (High score is 5.)

Ideas and Content: 3	**Sentence Fluency: 2**
Organization: 2	**Conventions: 1**
Voice: 2	**Presentation: 3**
Word Choice: 2	

Comments:

Ideas and Content: Although the essay's sequencing is predictably logical and its topic is focused, the writing is poorly developed. The vague position presented in the second paragraph is supported by a few relevant reasons; however, many of the overall supporting details are irrelevant and distracting. Sustained argument is absent.

Organization: Ideas are not presented in an effective order. The essay's position should appear in the introduction, but it instead appears in the concluding paragraph. Transitions to help connect ideas are missing.

Voice: The tone is overly informal. However, the writer reveals a personal dimension by indicating some experience with cafeteria overcrowding.

Word Choice: Words are generally adequate and correct, but they lack precision. Use of words such as *stuff* and the colloquial phrase *packed to the gills* detract from the editorial's effectiveness.

Sentence Fluency: Sentences are clear in meaning, but poor punctuation causes rambling, run-on sentences. Sentences lack variety in structure and length.

Conventions: The writing demonstrates a poor understanding of English-language conventions. Paragraphs are missing, and many errors exist in spelling, punctuation, and grammar.

Presentation: The presentation is simple but marred by erasures.

Holistic Scale
Response to Literature

Score 4

This insightful response to literature presents a thoroughly supported thesis and illustrates a comprehensive grasp of the text and the author's use of literary devices.

■ *The writing strongly demonstrates*

✓ a thoughtful, comprehensive understanding of the text

✓ support of the thesis and main ideas with specific textual details and examples that are accurate and coherent

✓ a thorough understanding of the text's ambiguities, nuances, and complexities

✓ a variety of sentence types using precise, descriptive language

✓ a clear understanding of the author's use of literary and stylistic devices

✓ a solid command of English-language conventions. Errors, if any, are generally minor and unobtrusive.

Score 3

This response to literature presents a clear thesis that is supported by details and examples.

■ *The writing generally demonstrates*

✓ a comprehensive understanding of the text

✓ support of the thesis and main ideas with general textual details and examples that are accurate and coherent

✓ an understanding of the text's ambiguities, nuances, and complexities

✓ a variety of sentence types using some descriptive language

✓ an understanding of the author's use of literary and stylistic devices

✓ an understanding of English-language conventions. Some errors exist, but they do not interfere with the reader's understanding of the essay.

Score 2

This literary response presents a thesis, but it is not sufficiently supported. The writing shows little understanding of the text.

■ *The writing demonstrates*

✓ a limited understanding of the text

✓ little, if any, support of the thesis and main ideas with textual details and examples

✓ limited, or no, understanding of the text's ambiguities, nuances, and complexities

✓ little variety in sentence types; use of basic, predictable language

✓ a limited understanding of the author's use of literary and stylistic devices

✓ inconsistent use of English-language conventions. Several errors exist and may interfere with the reader's understanding of the essay.

Holistic Scale
Response to Literature *(continued)*

Score 1

This literary response contains serious analytical and English-language errors. It shows no understanding of the text or of the author's use of literary devices.

- *The writing lacks*

  ✓ an understanding of the text
  ✓ textual details and examples to support the thesis and main ideas
  ✓ an understanding of the text's ambiguities, nuances, and complexities
  ✓ sentence variety and adequate vocabulary
  ✓ an understanding of the author's use of literary and stylistic devices
  ✓ an understanding of English-language conventions. (Serious errors interfere with the reader's understanding of the essay.)

Sample A: Response to Literature

PROMPT

Think of a short story you have read, and examine the story's parts—or literary elements—to find out how they work together to produce an overall effect and meaning. Then, write an analysis of the story to share with classmates.

Sometimes people get so wrapped up in what society thinks of them that they do foolish things. For instance, when my grandmother was a child, she won many piano contests and went to a state competition. But she became so nervous at the competition that she began shaking. She ended up lying to her parents, telling them that she had hurt her arm and couldn't play. She didn't want everyone to see how scared she was. Similarly, the self-absorbed main character in Guy de Maupassant's short story "A Coward" makes a tragic decision because he is so worried about what people think of him.

The main character, Viscount Gontran Joseph de Signoles, is handsome, confident, and well respected. Young women admire him, and young men envy him. The viscount is macho and aware of his talents, boasting that he'd "choose a pistol" in a fight. "With that weapon," he says, "I am sure of killing my man." Complications begin when the viscount takes some friends to a café. A strange man stares at one of the viscount's female friends. The woman is slightly bothered by this, but her husband shrugs off any offense. The viscount, however, becomes offended because he brought his friends to the café and because he is so self-centered. The viscount approaches the strange man and expresses his annoyance. The man curses loudly. With the eyes of everyone in the café upon them, the viscount responds by punching the stranger and challenging him to a duel. The men are separated, and the viscount returns home upset that this "beast," this "stranger, an unknown" had dared to be so rude and insolent.

Then the viscount makes a tragic decision. He feels that he has "done what he ought to do" at the café and that "people would talk of it, approve of it, and congratulate him," so he decides to go ahead and duel the stranger. He chooses two witnesses to aid

SCALES AND SAMPLE PAPERS

Sample A: Response to Literature *(continued)*

him in this duel—two men whose names "would carry in the journals." He also decides that although a duel with swords is less risky than with pistols, he wants pistols as "there was a chance of his adversary withdrawing." It is obvious that the viscount is more preoccupied with how his high-society peers will think of him than with the original "offense" committed by the stranger.

After he makes his decision to duel with pistols, the viscount begins unraveling. He trembles, thinking of his potential death the next day. Shivering, he almost rings his servant to light a fire but decides not to because the servant "would perceive at once that I am afraid." Although the viscount is still terrified, he forces himself the next day to contact the witnesses about the duel and repeats to himself, "I must prove that I am not afraid." The friends return with bad news—the stranger has agreed to the duel. Now the viscount feels he has no way out. He cannot stop shivering and thinks he is going crazy. "I cannot fight in this condition," he despairs. He thinks of "the laughs in the drawing-rooms, of the scorn of the ladies . . . of all the insults that cowards would throw at him." As he inspects his pistol and finds it loaded, he sees an escape and impulsively shoots himself rather than face the possibility of humiliation.

The irony of "A Coward" is that the self-centered viscount is so obsessed with his reputation that the thought of publicly losing it scares him more than the thought of death itself. "A Coward" invites us to reconsider the motivations behind our own self-centered actions and to recognize that being self-absorbed can lead us to make mistakes. If my grandmother had read this story, I am certain she would have reconsidered her decision to skip that piano competition!

Sample A Evaluation: Response to Literature

Holistic Scale

Rating: 4 points

Note: This essay illustrates the type of development appropriate for the prompt, but some teachers may ask their students for longer essays.

Comments: This is an insightful, well-written short story analysis. The analysis shows a thorough understanding of the text's complexities. The thesis is supported by relevant examples from the story, especially those that show the self-centeredness of the main character. Direct quotations from the story are woven skillfully into paragraphs. Sentence types are varied and use precise, descriptive language. The writing shows an excellent command of English-language conventions.

Analytical Scale: 6 Traits—Plus 1

Ratings (High score is 5.)

Ideas and Content: 5	**Sentence Fluency: 5**
Organization: 4	**Conventions: 5**
Voice: 5	**Presentation: 4**
Word Choice: 4	

Comments:

Ideas and Content: The thesis is well supported. The writing demonstrates a deep and thoughtful understanding of the text. The anecdote in the introductory paragraph leads the reader smoothly into the analysis.

Organization: Organization is clear, although the first body paragraph is too long. A clear thesis leads to thorough supporting evidence. The conclusion restates the thesis and contains a logical, thought-provoking comment.

Voice: The tone is appropriate for a literary analysis.

Word Choice: Precise, appropriate usage shows careful attention to vocabulary, although the colloquial expression *losing it* is too informal for an essay.

Sentence Fluency: Sentences are varied and well constructed. Dialogue is natural and purposeful.

Conventions: The writing shows an excellent command of grammar, usage, and mechanics.

Presentation: The presentation is simple and clear.

Sample B: Response to Literature

PROMPT

Think of a short story you have read, and examine the story's parts—or literary elements—to find out how they work together to produce an overall effect and meaning. Then, write an analysis of the story to share with classmates.

"It's all about me!" Have you ever heard someone say this? Some people are really self centered and think everything is about them. In the short story "A Coward," the main character is so full of himself that he makes a terrible choice.

The main character, Viscount Signoles, is good looking and everyone in society likes him. He is kind of macho and he boasted that if he was ever in a fight he would use a gun because he would be "sure of killing my man."

One day the Viscount takes some friends to a café. A man stares at one of the Viscount's female friends and this makes the Viscount mad because he brought his friends to the café to begin with and because he is so self centered. The Viscount and the man end up fighting. Then the Viscount makes a tragic decision. He decides that although everyone approved of his fight at the café he needs to go a step farther and challenge the stranger to a duel with pistols.

After he makes his decision to duel with pistols, the Viscount starts going totally nuts. He is shaking with fear—he is afraid he will be dead tomorrow. "I cannot fight in this condition," he thinks. He starts thinking of how other people will think of him if they see him shaking during the duel: "the laughs in the drawing-rooms, of the scorn of the ladies." So instead he decides to kill himself so he doesn't have to deal with people making fun of him. He shoots himself and the blood sprays all over his will: "This is my testament."

The Viscount ends up paying a terrible price for his self centered nature in "A Coward." It's strange to think that the story is called "A Coward" when the Viscount had no problem killing himself. That's why this story is ironic. People who are self absorbed need to think about the Viscount before they make a mistake in their life, because life is NOT all about them!

SCALES AND SAMPLE PAPERS

Sample B Evaluation: Response to Literature

Holistic Scale

Rating: 3 points

Comments: This analysis has a somewhat clear thesis that is supported by general textual details. The writing shows an adequate understanding of the events of the story and what those events represent. Sentence types are varied but lack precision. The writer uses a few direct quotations, but at least one quotation is irrelevant to the essay's purpose. The writing shows an understanding of English-language conventions, though some errors exist in punctuation and spelling.

Analytical Scale: 6 Traits—Plus 1

Ratings (High score is 5.)

Ideas and Content: 2	**Sentence Fluency: 3**
Organization: 4	**Conventions: 3**
Voice: 2	**Presentation: 4**
Word Choice: 2	

Comments:

Ideas and Content: The thesis is clear but would have benefited from the writer's deeper understanding of the story. Key points lack adequate support. The introductory quote—"It's all about me!"—is successful in getting the audience's attention but does not lead us to a meaningful understanding of the main character. The essay's writer never identifies the author of the short story.

Organization: The analysis contains a clear introduction with a thesis, a clearly organized body, and a conclusion that restates the thesis and summarizes content. However, the conclusion ends with a weak, thoughtlessly uninspiring comment.

Voice: The tone, although relatively consistent, is overly informal for a response to literature.

Word Choice: Word choice is adequate, but informal words such as *nuts* detract from the essay's purpose. Common nouns, adjectives, and verbs could be replaced by more precise, descriptive words.

Sentence Fluency: Sentences are varied in length but occasionally run on. More frequent, perceptive use of quotations would improve the essay.

Conventions: The essay contains errors in punctuation, spelling, and grammar.

Presentation: The presentation is clear.

STUDENT MODEL

Sample C: Response to Literature

PROMPT

Think of a short story you have read, and examine the story's parts—or literary elements—to find out how they work together to produce an overall effect and meaning. Then, write an analysis of the story to share with classmates.

The main character in Guy Maupsant's short story "Coward," does not realize he's really depressed until the end of the story when he kills himself. He should have gotten some therapy instead of killing himself. This story is a cry for help for everyone.

The main character is a vicount and he is handsome and popular. But you never know what is going on deep inside someone. Even though everyone likes him nobody really knows him. They don't know that when he challenges some guy to a duel that he is really afraid of fighting. He becomes so depressed he shoots himself instead of dueling this other man.

The vicount takes his friends to a café to eat some ice. They had been to the theater before that. A stranger is staring at his friend which makes him angry. They get in a fight.

The vicount doesn't really want to duel. He feels "no emotion whatever" which is a sign of depression. I cannot fight in this condition" he says. George Lamil is the name of the man he is going to fight. Who was this man? Says the vicount. He is jitery before the fight and can't sleep. Loosing sleep is another sign of depression. Then he starts drinking rum and finishes the whole bottle. Many alcholics are depressed. He asks "What is going to become of me?"

People should recognize the signs of depression so they can help there friends. The poor vicount had freinds but no one saw the signs and he didn't have a hotline to call because this story takes place a long time ago. "Coward" is a sad story about people not recognizing the signs of suicide. Everyone needs to pay closer attention to the behavoir of people who kill themselves so they can stop it.

SCALES AND SAMPLE PAPERS

Sample C Evaluation: Response to Literature

Holistic Scale

Rating: 2 points

Comments: This analysis is poorly developed and often vague. Although supporting evidence is present, the thesis shows that the writer did not adequately grasp the story's underlying meaning. Sentences sometimes vary in structure, but they are usually basic. Errors exist in grammar, punctuation, and usage.

Analytical Scale: 6 Traits—Plus 1

Ratings (High score is 5.)

Ideas and Content: 2	**Sentence Fluency: 2**
Organization: 2	**Conventions: 1**
Voice: 2	**Presentation: 3**
Word Choice: 2	

Comments:

Ideas and Content: Although supporting evidence supports the thesis, it is clear that the writer does not clearly understand the short story.

Organization: The introduction and conclusion are present but contain irrelevant points and suggestions and include a misspelling of the author's name and an inaccurate rendering of the story's title. The essay does not relate the story's events in chronological order. The conclusion ends with a weak and illogical comment.

Voice: The tone is generally appropriate, although somewhat informal.

Word Choice: The language is vague and imprecise. Pronoun reference is frequently unclear.

Sentence Fluency: Sentences are monotonous and poorly constructed. Use of quotations is limited but effective.

Conventions: The essay contains serious errors in punctuation, spelling, and grammar.

Presentation: The presentation is clear.

Holistic Scale
Persuasion

Score 4

This persuasive writing presents a clear position and supports the position with precise, relevant evidence. The reader's concerns, biases, and expectations are addressed convincingly.

- *The writing strongly demonstrates*
  - ✓ a clear understanding of all parts of the writing task
  - ✓ a meaningful thesis, a consistent tone and focus, and a purposeful control of organization
  - ✓ use of specific details and examples to support the thesis and main ideas
  - ✓ a variety of sentence types using precise, descriptive language
  - ✓ a clear understanding of audience
  - ✓ use of precise, relevant evidence to defend a position with authority, convincingly addressing the reader's concerns, biases, and expectations
  - ✓ a solid command of English-language conventions. Errors, if any, are generally minor and unobtrusive.

Score 3

This persuasive writing presents a position and supports it with evidence. The reader's concerns are addressed.

- *The writing generally demonstrates*
  - ✓ an understanding of all parts of the writing task
  - ✓ a thesis, a consistent tone and focus, and a control of organization
  - ✓ use of details and examples to support the thesis and main ideas
  - ✓ a variety of sentence types using some descriptive language
  - ✓ an understanding of audience
  - ✓ use of relevant evidence to defend a position, addressing the reader's concerns, biases, and expectations
  - ✓ an understanding of English-language conventions. Some errors exist, but they do not interfere with the reader's understanding of the essay.

Score 2

This persuasive writing presents a position, but the position is not sufficiently supported.

- *The writing demonstrates*
  - ✓ an understanding of only parts of the writing task
  - ✓ a weak thesis; an inconsistent tone and focus; and little, if any, control of organization
  - ✓ use of limited, if any, details and examples to support the thesis and main ideas
  - ✓ few, if any, sentence types and use of basic, predictable language
  - ✓ little or no understanding of audience

Holistic Scale
Persuasion *(continued)*

✓ use of little, if any, evidence to defend a position. The reader's concerns, biases, and expectations are not effectively addressed.

✓ inconsistent use of English-language conventions. Several errors exist and may interfere with the reader's understanding of the essay.

Score 1

This persuasive writing may
present a position, but it
is not supported.

- *The writing lacks*

✓ an understanding of the writing task, addressing only one part

✓ a thesis (or provides only a weak thesis), a focus, and control of organization

✓ details and examples to support ideas

✓ sentence variety and effective vocabulary

✓ an understanding of audience

✓ evidence to defend a position and a successful attempt to address the reader's concerns, biases, and expectations

✓ an understanding of English-language conventions. (Serious errors interfere with the reader's understanding of the essay.)

Sample A: Persuasion

PROMPT

When was the last time you disagreed with someone over an important issue? How did you try to persuade him or her to agree with you? Write a persuasive essay using relevant evidence to defend a position you feel strongly about, and share your essay with a friend. Remember to address possible biases.

If you could, wouldn't you want to increase students' chances of getting into a top university or finding a good job? One way to do this is to increase students' fluency in a second language. Two years of study of another language should be a graduation requirement.

I know what you're thinking: Not only do students have too many graduation requirements, but they also will resent another language requirement when anyone who wants to take extra language courses can do so already.

The truth is that most students can get diplomas without studying any language other than English. Many students will not choose to take a language elective when they can choose something easier. They will limit their choice of jobs and the universities or colleges to which they can apply. Some of the best universities require at least two years of a language other than English before they will even consider an application. Lots of students wait until their senior year in high school to think about college. By then, if they haven't studied another language, they've already lost the chance to enter some of the top universities.

However, it isn't just college-bound students who have limited their options. Lots of jobs require fluency in a second language. The language varies from area to area, but Spanish and Vietnamese are required for quite a few jobs in parts of the United States. Ads often list a second language as "desirable," meaning that job applicants who know a second language are more likely to be hired.

Police officers and firefighters in large cities are often paid more if they are fluent in a language spoken by significant numbers of people in the communities they serve. For example, bilingual police officers in Houston, Texas, receive a pay

Sample A: Persuasion (continued)

supplement for their language skills. Bilingual firefighters in Phoenix, Arizona, receive $100 extra per month. In a tight job market it's good to know another language.

Learning another language would also improve students' English. Studying the grammar, sentence structure, and vocabulary of another language often helps people better understand English. My father told me that he did not understand the subjunctive in English until he studied French. Similarly, my uncle Abraham said that studying Italian increased his English vocabulary.

Even though English is spoken by many well-educated people in all countries, we ought to make an effort to learn the languages spoken in other nations. Doing so would increase our understanding of their cultures and would help us avoid cultural misunderstandings. Being able to speak and understand another language could turn each of us into a goodwill ambassador for the United States.

Some people are worried that if states require students to study a second language for two years, those of us who want to take elective classes such as drama, band, and art will be unable to take those classes for those two years. However, I think schools will be able to adjust to this requirement by adding classes in the early-morning period, before the regular schedule. Many schools, including ours, already have electives that begin in the early period. Currently I take Orchestra in the early-morning period. Students who want to take electives will have the valuable experience of learning a second language in exchange for getting to school a little earlier.

Adding a second-language requirement will help prepare students for more jobs and for higher-education opportunities, and it will also help Americans better communicate with people from other cultures. Let's learn another language and become better citizens of the world—and of our own country.

Sample A Evaluation: Persuasion

Holistic Scale

Rating: 4 points

Note: This essay illustrates the type of development appropriate for the prompt, but some teachers may ask their students for longer essays.

Comments: This persuasive essay shows that the writer has a clear understanding of all parts of the writing task. The introduction presents a clear position, which is supported by relevant reasons and evidence. The possible objection to lost electives is sufficiently addressed by presenting an option for early-morning classes. The tone and focus are appropriate and consistent. Precise, descriptive language is used, and sentences are varied in length and structure. The writing shows a strong command of English-language conventions.

Analytical Scale: 6 Traits—Plus 1

Ratings (High score is 5.)

Ideas and Content: 5	**Sentence Fluency: 5**
Organization: 4	**Conventions: 5**
Voice: 5	**Presentation: 4**
Word Choice: 4	

Comments:

Ideas and Content: The topic is clearly focused. Original ideas, including the reference to pay rates for bilingual police officers and firefighters, are used to discuss a topical issue. The writer is obviously writing from personal knowledge and experience.

Organization: Ideas are presented in a logical and effective order. The essay includes a clear introduction and conclusion. Transitions are used effectively to connect ideas but are sometimes absent.

Voice: The tone is appropriately sincere without sounding overly formal or academic. The writer reveals a personal dimension by presenting examples of her family's experience with learning a second language. The writer shows a strong connection to the topic and explains how learning a second language could be beneficial for all high school students.

Word Choice: Words are specific and appropriate. The language is natural and is relatively free of jargon and clichés.

Sentence Fluency: Sentences are clear in meaning and varied in length and structure.

Conventions: The writing shows a strong command of English-language conventions.

Presentation: The presentation is simple and clear.

Sample B: Persuasion

PROMPT

When was the last time you disagreed with someone over an important issue? How did you try to persuade him or her to agree with you? Write a persuasive essay using relevant evidence to defend a position you feel strongly about, and share your essay with a friend. Remember to address possible biases.

Getting a good job is important for students, and they are more likely to get good jobs if they study a second language. Even low-level jobs require a second language. Students should have to study at least two years of a language other than English. If not, they should not be allowed to graduate.

Some people think students already have to many subjects to study. Students can already take extra language courses, and there's no need for everyone to learn "parlay vous fransay."

Many universities require at least two years of a second language. If students wait until their senior year to take language classes, their ship has sunk. They won't enter a top university.

It isn't just college-bound students who are kicking themselves. Lots of jobs require people to speak a second language. Spanish and Vietnamese are required for a bunch of jobs in the U.S. Police officers can get paid more money if they speak other languages. For example, officers in Texas receive more money for speaking Spanish. English is spoken by lots of people all over the world. But students should try to learn other languages; that would help them understand other cultures.

Some folks are worried that if students have to study a second language for two years, they won't be able to take electives. Students can still take these classes but in the early-morning period where classes like band or orchestra begin at 7:00.

Adding a second-language requirement for high schoolers will help them get better jobs. This requirment will also help Americans understand people from other cultures. These people could be over seas or even right here in the good old U.S. of A.!

Sample B Evaluation: Persuasion

Holistic Scale	**Rating: 3 points**

Comments: This persuasive essay shows that the writer has a general understanding of most parts of the writing task. The introduction presents a clear position, but insufficient reasons and evidence are used to support the position. The possible objection to lost electives is sufficiently addressed by presenting an option for early-morning classes. The tone and focus are consistent; however, the essay's language is fairly colloquial. Language is generally adequate, but some sentences lack transitions. The writing shows a general understanding of English-language conventions.

Analytical Scale: 6 Traits—Plus 1

Ratings (High score is 5.)

Ideas and Content: 3	**Sentence Fluency: 3**
Organization: 4	**Conventions: 3**
Voice: 3	**Presentation: 4**
Word Choice: 3	

Comments:

Ideas and Content: The topic is clearly focused. However, ideas are not very original, and the cited example is not well developed. The writing does not show that the writer is arguing the position from personal knowledge or experience.

Organization: Ideas are presented in a logical and effective order. The essay includes a clear introduction and conclusion. However, a lack of transitions makes the essay choppy and sometimes confusing.

Voice: The tone is appropriately sincere but somewhat informal. However, the writing does not reveal a personal dimension; it is too detached.

Word Choice: Words are generally adequate and correct, but clichés such as *their ship has sunk* and colloquial phrases such as *kicking themselves* detract from the essay's effectiveness.

Sentence Fluency: Sentences are clear in meaning but are routine rather than artful. Sentence beginnings lack variety, and the reader is sometimes forced to search for transitions that help make connections between ideas.

Conventions: The writing shows a general understanding of English-language conventions. Although there are problems with spelling, only minor errors exist in spelling, punctuation, and grammar.

Presentation: The presentation is simple and clear.

SCALES AND SAMPLE PAPERS

Sample C: Persuasion

PROMPT

When was the last time you disagreed with someone over an important issue? How did you try to persuade him or her to agree with you? Write a persuasive essay using relevant evidence to defend a position you feel strongly about, and share your essay with a friend. Remember to address possible biases.

People think English is the only langauge worth speaking. Americans go into China and speak English and then get mad when the chinese people don't know English. Whatever! That atitude is not fare, we shouldn't expect chinese folks to know English! It's very important for high schoolers to take a langauge other than English. You can take French, Spanish, Latin, and German and even Italin at my school. You can take these languages and then get into a good College.

Students need at least two years of studying another langauge before gradation. You can make more cash that way because all kinds of jobs want two langauges. And Colleges they want students who speak diffrent langauges. So take those classes and learn some Spanish! It can't hurt it can only help you.

A lot of jobs now want Spainish speakers. And my freind in Houston says they want chinese down there also. So sometimes you need to know three langauges in order to get a job. Some folks say high schoolers are really busy and don't have time to take Spainish. Well if high schoolers want to be flippin burgers when their adults than let them!

Sample C Evaluation: Persuasion

Holistic Scale

Rating: 2 points
Comments: This persuasive essay is poorly organized and shows that the writer does not understand all parts of the writing task. The introduction presents a reason before stating the vague position near the end of the first paragraph. A possible bias is mentioned in the final two sentences, but it is addressed with a potentially offensive personal opinion. The writing shows a poor understanding of English-language conventions.

Analytical Scale: 6 Traits—Plus 1

Ratings (High score is 5.)

Ideas and Content: 2	**Sentence Fluency: 2**
Organization: 1	**Conventions: 1**
Voice: 2	**Presentation: 4**
Word Choice: 2	

Comments:

Ideas and Content: The topic is unfocused and undeveloped. The vague position presented in the introduction lacks relevant reasons and specific evidence. The writer presents examples drawn from personal experience, but some examples are undeveloped and appear to be digressive.

Organization: Ideas are not presented in a logical and effective order. The call to action, located in the second paragraph, belongs in the closing.

Voice: The tone is far too informal and flippant for an essay.

Word Choice: While words are generally clear, slang words such as *whatever* and clichés such as "It can't hurt it can only help you" are inappropriate for a persuasive essay.

Sentence Fluency: Sentence meanings are generally clear, but poor punctuation leads to awkward comma splices and fused sentences. Sentences lack variety in structure and length.

Conventions: The writing shows a poor understanding of English-language conventions. Many errors exist in spelling, grammar, and punctuation.

Presentation: The presentation is simple and clear.

Holistic Scale
Business Letter

Score 4

This business letter provides clear, purposeful information. Conventional business-letter style contributes to readability and overall effect. The tone is consistent and appropriate for the intended audience.

- *The writing strongly demonstrates*

  ✓ a clear understanding of all parts of the writing task
  ✓ a meaningful message, a consistent tone and focus, and a purposeful control of organization
  ✓ use of specific details and examples to support the main purpose
  ✓ a variety of sentence types using precise, descriptive language
  ✓ a clear understanding of audience
  ✓ a thorough understanding of conventional business-letter style, with formats, fonts, and spacing that aid readability and have a positive overall effect
  ✓ a solid command of English-language conventions. Errors, if any, are minor and unobtrusive.

Score 3

This business letter provides clear information. Conventional business-letter style generally contributes to readability. The tone is appropriate for the intended audience.

- *The writing generally demonstrates*

  ✓ an understanding of all parts of the writing task
  ✓ a clear message, a consistent tone and focus, and a control of organization
  ✓ use of details and examples to support the purpose
  ✓ a variety of sentence types using some descriptive language
  ✓ an understanding of audience
  ✓ an understanding of conventional business-letter style, with formats, fonts, and spacing that aid readability and have a positive overall effect
  ✓ an understanding of English-language conventions. Some errors exist, but they do not interfere with the reader's understanding of the letter.

Score 2

This business letter provides somewhat vague information and strays from its focus. Conventional business-letter style is not used consistently, leaving a negative overall impression.

- *The writing demonstrates*

  ✓ an understanding of only parts of the writing task
  ✓ a weak message; an inconsistent tone and focus; and little, if any, control of organization
  ✓ use of limited, if any, details and examples to support the purpose
  ✓ little variety in sentence types and use of basic, predictable language
  ✓ little or no understanding of audience

Holistic Scale
Business Letter *(continued)*

✓ little understanding of conventional business-letter style. Formats, fonts, and spacing sometimes impede readability.

✓ inconsistent use of English-language conventions. Several errors exist and may interfere with the reader's understanding of the letter.

Score 1

This business letter shows no understanding of business-letter purpose or style. The tone is inappropriate for the audience. Incorrect style and serious grammatical errors greatly impede readability and have an overall negative effect.

- *The writing lacks*

✓ an understanding of the writing task, addressing only one part

✓ a clear message, a focus, and control of organization

✓ details and examples to support the purpose

✓ sentence variety and effective vocabulary

✓ an understanding of audience

✓ an understanding of conventional business-letter style. (Formats, fonts, and spacing impede readability and have a negative overall effect.)

✓ an understanding of English-language conventions. (Serious errors interfere with the reader's understanding of the letter.)

Sample A: Business Letter

PROMPT

When you apply for a job, your cover letter can help determine whether your résumé is taken seriously. Think of a job you would like to have, and write a business letter that you would send along with your résumé when applying for the job. Remember to use conventional business-letter format.

7008 Canyon Way
Austin, TX 78705
May 12, 2005

Ms. Samantha Martinez, Manager
Americana Cinema 4
4362 Bluebonnet Blvd.
Austin, TX 78757

Dear Ms. Martinez:

I am writing in response to the *Austin American-Statesman* classified advertisement for openings at the Americana Cinema 4. As a worker with previous food and beverage experience, I am interested in interviewing for a position on your staff. I think I could be a valuable part of the team.

For the past two summers I have worked as a snow cone maker and cashier at Sally's Snow Cones on Barton Springs Road. My job responsibilities included making snow cones, operating the cash register, checking inventory on syrup and cups, and cleaning the ice machine on a daily basis. Occasionally I also performed maintenance on the ice machine when it jammed.

Currently, I am an honors student at Independence High School here in Austin. My coursework, above and beyond classes in the standard curriculum, includes honors classes in language arts and mathematics. I have also taken elective courses in business economics and marketing, play alto saxophone in the high school band, and serve as a photographer on the yearbook staff.

Sample A: Business Letter *(continued)*

I would be glad to meet with you for an interview to discuss my qualifications further. I have included my contact information on the enclosed job application. I can also provide reference letters if you need them.

Thank you very much for your consideration. I look forward to hearing from you soon.

Sincerely,

Kari DeBauge

Kari DeBauge

Sample A Evaluation: Business Letter

Holistic Scale	**Rating: 4 points**

Comments: This business letter shows that the writer has a strong understanding of all aspects of business-letter writing. The letter is focused, well written, and well organized. Specific details and examples are used to support the writer's main point. The letter retains a formal, courteous tone throughout. The block-style format is appropriate and is used consistently, and English-language conventions are strictly observed.

Analytical Scale: 6 Traits—Plus 1

Ratings (High score is 5.)

Ideas and Content: 4	**Sentence Fluency: 5**
Organization: 5	**Conventions: 5**
Voice: 5	**Presentation: 5**
Word Choice: 4	

Comments:

Ideas and Content: The letter never strays from its focus. The writer is obviously writing from personal experience. Details are insightful and well considered.

Organization: Block-style format is correctly and consistently used. The first paragraph succinctly states the purpose of the letter, the second paragraph provides supporting details, and the closing includes a courteous note of appreciation.

Voice: The tone is appropriately formal and consistent.

Word Choice: Words are specific and appropriate. The language is natural.

Sentence Fluency: Well-crafted sentences ensure a letter that is clear and easy to read. Sentences vary in length and structure. Transitions help the reader make connections between ideas.

Conventions: The letter shows a strong command of English-language conventions.

Presentation: The presentation is simple, clear, and appropriate for a business letter.

Sample B: Business Letter

PROMPT

When you apply for a job, your cover letter can help determine whether your résumé is taken seriously. Think of a job you would like to have, and write a business letter that you would send along with your résumé when applying for the job. Remember to use conventional business-letter format.

7008 Canyon Way
Austin, TX 78705
May 12, 2005

Americana Cinema 4
4362 Bluebonnet Blvd.
Austin, TX 78757

Dear Americana Cinema 4:

After seeing your "Help Wanted" ad in the newspaper, I decided to let you know that I'd love to work at your theater. I have been watching movies at your theater since it opened in 1998 and I gotta say the politeness and helpfulness of your staff is totally amazing. I think I could really help you out this summer.

For the past two summers I have worked at Sally's Snow Cones on Barton Springs Road. I made lots of snow cones and took people's money. Customer's loved me because I hardly forgot anyone's order—I have a really good memory! I also counted all the cups and syrup bottles every night so we could order more if we needed them. Sometimes the ice machine got jammed and I had to fix it and my boss was like "Kari, you got some nimble fingers!"

Right now I'm a student at Independence High School here in Austin. I'm taking classes in language arts, math, science, and health. I also play saxophone in the school band, and I sometimes help out on the school newspaper: I get to go out and find businesses—like Americana Cinema—that will buy space for ads.

Sample B: Business Letter *(continued)*

I would be thrilled to chat with you about the job! Give me a call—my digits are on the job application I picked up at the box office.

Thanks a lot for looking this over. I can't wait to hear from you! See you at the movies!

Kari DeBauge

Kari DeBauge

Sample B Evaluation: Business Letter

Holistic Scale

Rating: 3 points

Comments: This business letter shows that the writer has a vague understanding of aspects of business-letter writing. The letter is clear and organized, though the salutation and closing are inappropriate. The tone is overly familiar for a business letter, and some language is too colloquial. With the exception of indented paragraphs, block-style format is used correctly. The writing shows a good understanding of English-language conventions.

Analytical Scale: 6 Traits—Plus 1

Ratings (High score is 5.)

Ideas and Content: 4	**Sentence Fluency: 4**
Organization: 4	**Conventions: 3**
Voice: 2	**Presentation: 4**
Word Choice: 3	

Comments:

Ideas and Content: The letter is focused, and the writer is writing from personal experience.

Organization: Block-style format is correctly used, with the exception of the indented paragraphs. Sentences and paragraphs flow logically from one to the next.

Voice: The tone is too informal for a business letter.

Word Choice: Words are generally specific, but words like *gotta* and *digits* and phrases like *totally amazing* and *my boss was like* are inappropriate.

Sentence Fluency: Sentences vary in length and structure. Transitions help the reader make connections between ideas.

Conventions: While the letter contains errors in punctuation, it shows a command of English-language conventions.

Presentation: The presentation is simple, clear, and relatively appropriate.

Sample C: Business Letter

PROMPT

When you apply for a job, your cover letter can help determine whether your résumé is taken seriously. Think of a job you would like to have, and write a business letter that you would send along with your résumé when applying for the job. Remember to use conventional business-letter format.

7008 Canyon Way

Austin, TX 78705

May 12, 2005

Ms. Samantha Martinez, Manager

Americana Cinema 4

4362 Bluebonnet Blvd.

Austin, TX 78757

Hey Samantha,

I love to watch movies so much. I'm jealous you get to watch so many cool flicks! I have a collection of 73 DVDs and 154 video casettes. My mom said she's tired of them cluttering up the house, so I just hide them under my bed. Anyways, I saw your ad in the paper yesterday. I'd love to work at a movie theater! Last summer and the one before that I worked at a snowcone place near Zilker Park— heard of Sally's Snowcones? Well that's where I worked! I made lots of diffrent kinds of snowcones—rainbow snowcones, ebony and ivory snowcones (that's licorish and vanila), sunshine snowcones (bannana, lemon, and mango), and so many others I'll have to tell ya about them later cuz I'm running out of room here! The customers loved me—they were always telling me I was an artist, my cones looked so pretty! Sometimes I had to fix the ice machine which wuz scary. I want to work at the theater because I love movies so much. I might even love popcorn more than snowcones! Give me a call on my cell when your ready to interview me! Thanks!

Kari DeBauge

Sample C Evaluation: Business Letter

Holistic Scale

Rating: 2 points

Comments: This letter shows that the writer has little understanding of business-letter writing. The letter is poorly written, poorly organized, and inappropriate in tone. Although the format is block style, the letter is handwritten, and some elements are incorrect or incomplete. The writing shows a poor understanding of English-language conventions.

Analytical Scale: 6 Traits—Plus 1

Ratings (High score is 5.)

Ideas and Content: 2	**Sentence Fluency:** 3
Organization: 1	**Conventions:** 2
Voice: 1	**Presentation:** 2
Word Choice: 2	

Comments:

Ideas and Content: The letter is poorly focused, containing much irrelevant information.

Organization: The letter contains a single, rambling paragraph. The purpose of the letter is not clear until the fifth sentence.

Voice: The letter shows no concern for audience. The tone is far too informal for a business letter.

Word Choice: While words are generally clear, slang words and phrases such as *cool flicks*, *ya*, and *wuz* are inappropriate for a business letter.

Sentence Fluency: Sentence meanings are generally clear, but sentences lack variety in structure.

Conventions: The letter contains numerous errors in spelling, grammar, and punctuation. The letter overuses exclamation points.

Presentation: The presentation is simple and clear, but the letter is handwritten.

Portfolio Assessment

Portfolio Assessment in the Language Arts

Although establishing and using a portfolio assessment system requires a certain amount of time, effort, and understanding, many teachers believe that the benefits of implementing such a system richly reward their efforts.

Language arts portfolios are collections of materials that display aspects of students' use of language so that they and their teachers can ascertain how the students are developing as language users. Because reflection and self-assessment are aspects of language arts portfolios, portfolios also help students develop their critical-thinking and metacognitive abilities.

Each portfolio collection is typically kept in a folder, box, or other container to which items are added on a regular basis. Many portfolios include several versions of the same piece of writing and show development through revision. However, the collection can include a great variety of materials. For example, portfolios may contain student stories, essays, sketches, poems, letters, journals, and other original writing, as well as reactions to articles, stories, and other texts. Students may also include drawings, photographs, audio and video recordings of special activities, clippings and pictures from newspapers and magazines, and notes on favorite authors, stories, and books.

Finally, portfolios may contain reading or writing logs, written assessments of portfolio work, and tables and explanations about the portfolio's organization. (A collection of these forms may be found at the end of this book.)

The Advantages of Portfolio Assessment

Here are some important advantages of using portfolios:

- **Portfolios link instruction and assessment.** Traditional testing is usually removed from the process or performance being assessed. However, portfolio assessment focuses on performance—on students' actual use of language. Therefore, portfolios are a highly accurate gauge of what students have learned.

- **Portfolios involve students in assessing their own language use and abilities.** Portfolio assessment can provide effective learning opportunities, and assessment is itself instructional: Students, as self-assessors, identify their own strengths and weaknesses. Furthermore, portfolios are a natural way to develop metacognition in students. As students begin to think critically about how they make meaning while reading, writing, speaking, and listening, they begin to ask questions, such as "Is this telling me what I need to know?" "Am I enjoying this author as much as I expected to?" "Why or why not?" "Am I thinking about the goals I set when I was analyzing my portfolio?"

- **Portfolios invite attention to important aspects of language.** Because most portfolios include numerous writing samples, they direct attention to diction, style,

Portfolio Assessment in the Language Arts *(continued)*

As they become attuned to audience, students automatically begin to be more focused on whether their work has fulfilled their purpose for writing. They begin to ask questions like "Did I say what I meant to say?" "Could I have been clearer and more effective?" "Do I understand what this writer wants to tell me?" "Do I agree with it?" Speaking and listening activities can also be evaluated in terms of audience awareness and clarity of purpose.

main idea or theme, author's purpose, and other aspects of language that are sometimes difficult to assess.

- ***Portfolios emphasize language use as a process that integrates language behaviors.*** Students who keep and analyze portfolios develop an understanding that reading, writing, speaking, and listening are all aspects of a larger process.

- ***Portfolios make students aware of audience and the need for a writing purpose.*** Evaluation forms prompt students to reflect on whether they have defined and appropriately addressed an audience. Moreover, because portfolios support opportunities for students to work together, peers can often provide feedback about how well a student has addressed an audience. Finally, students may be asked to consider particular audiences (parents, classmates, or community groups, for example) for portfolio review; they may prepare explanations of contents and select specific papers for presentation to such audiences.

- ***Portfolios provide a vehicle for student interaction and cooperative learning.*** Many projects involving group learning produce material for portfolios. Portfolios, in turn, provide or support opportunities for students to work together in groups that critique each other's collections.

- ***Portfolios can incorporate many types of student expression on a variety of topics.*** Students should be encouraged to include materials from different subject areas and from outside school, especially materials related to hobbies and other special interests. In this way, students come to see language arts skills as crucial tools for authentic, real-world work.

- ***Portfolios provide genuine opportunities to learn about students and their progress as language users.*** Portfolio contents can reveal a great deal about a student's reading, writing, speaking, and listening background and interests. Portfolios can also demonstrate a student's development as a language user and reveal areas needing improvement.

How to Develop and Use Portfolios

As you begin designing a portfolio program for your students, you may wish to read articles and reports that discuss the advantages of portfolio assessment.

You may want to require that certain papers, projects, and reports be included in the portfolio. Such requirements should be kept to a minimum so that students feel that they can include whatever they consider to be relevant to their language development.

Portfolios that include such planning papers and intermediate drafts are called *working portfolios*. Working portfolios encourage the student to organize and analyze the material collected, activities that make clear to the student that language use is a process.

The act of selecting particular papers to show to special audiences—parents, another teacher, or the principal, to name a few—refines students' sense of audience. Preparing and presenting selected collections, called *show portfolios*, engages students in a more sophisticated analysis of their work and encourages them to visualize the audience for the show collection.

Basic Design Features

For a portfolio program to be successful in the classroom, the program should reflect the teacher's particular instructional goals and the students' needs as learners. While teachers are encouraged to customize a portfolio program for their classrooms, most successful portfolio programs share a core of essential portfolio management techniques. Consider the following suggestions:

- *Integrate portfolio assessment into the regular classroom routine.* Make portfolio work a regular class activity by providing opportunities for students to work with their collections during class time. During these portfolio sessions, promote analysis (assessment) that reflects your instructional objectives and goals.
- *Link the program to classroom activities.* Student portfolios should contain numerous examples of classroom activities and projects.
- *Let students have the control.* When students take ownership of their work, they accept more responsibility for their own language development. To encourage a sense of student ownership, store portfolios where students can get at them easily. Students should have regular and frequent access to their portfolios.
- *Include students' creative efforts.* To ensure that the portfolios develop a range of language skills, encourage students to include samples of their creative writing, outside writing, and publishing activities.
- *Make sure portfolios record students' writing process.* Portfolios should contain papers that show how writing grows out of planning and develops through revision. They should include notes, outlines, clippings, and reactions to materials that inspired the final product. They should also include different drafts of papers to demonstrate revision over a period of time. Such collections can promote fruitful, concrete discussions about how process has shaped the final product.
- *Rely on reactions to reading and listening.* Encourage students to include reactions to things they read and hear. During conferences, you may want to point out how some of the student's work has grown out of listening or reading.
- *Encourage students to consider the audience.* Prompt students to think about audience because, as a kind of publication, the portfolio invites a variety of readers. Help students become sensitive to the reactions of their classmates, their teachers, and other audiences that may view their portfolios.

How to Develop and Use Portfolios *(continued)*

If students feel free to include writing and reading done outside class in their portfolios, you can discover interests, opinions, and concerns that can be touched on during conferences. In turn, by communicating interest in and respect for what engages the student, you can promote the success of the portfolio program.

Some key considerations for designing a portfolio program have been suggested. Other considerations will arise as you assess ways to use the portfolios. Here are some questions that will probably arise in the planning stages of portfolio assessment.

How can I introduce students to the concepts of portfolio management?

What examples of student work should go into the portfolios?

What should the criteria be for deciding what will be included?

How and where will the portfolio collections be kept?

- *Promote collaborative products.* Consider promoting student collaboration by setting aside class time for students to react to one another's work and to work in groups. This interaction can occur informally or in more structured student partnerships or team activities. Many writing projects can be done by teams and small groups, and common products can be reproduced for all participants' portfolios. Performance projects, speeches, and other cooperative presentations may be included in portfolios as audio and video recordings.
- *Let the portfolios reflect a variety of subject areas and interests.* The language arts portfolio should include material from other subject areas. Broadening the portfolio beyond the language arts classroom helps students understand that reading, writing, speaking, and listening are real-world activities.

Designing a Portfolio Program

How can I introduce students to the concepts of portfolio management?

One way to introduce students to portfolios is to experiment with a group of your students. Select students with varied writing abilities to get a sense of how portfolios work for students with a range of skill levels. Then, talk to students either individually or as a group about what they will be doing. If other students begin expressing an interest in keeping portfolios, let them take part as well.

Once you have a clear idea of your teaching objectives, you might let students help you design or at least plan some details of the system. After explaining both the reasons for keeping portfolios and the essential elements of your program, you can let students discuss how they think certain aspects should be handled.

What examples of student work should go into the portfolios?

Portfolios should reflect the spectrum of your students' language use. Student self-assessment should lead to the understanding that language skills are essential to all learning. For this to happen, portfolios should contain writing, speaking, and listening activities that relate to a number of subject areas and interests, as well as drafts, notes, freewriting, and other samples that show a student's thinking and writing process.

FINAL PRODUCTS Students should consider including pieces that are created with a general audience in mind; writing that is intended for particular audiences; and personal writing used to think through situations, evaluate experiences, or muse for

How to Develop and Use Portfolios *(continued)*

enjoyment. Portfolios can contain a variety of finished products, including

- original stories, dialogue, and scripts
- poems
- essays, themes, sketches
- song lyrics
- original videos
- video or audio recordings of performances
- narrative accounts of experiences
- correspondence with family members and friends
- stream-of-consciousness pieces
- journals of various types

FRAGMENTS AND WORKS IN PROGRESS Portfolios should include, in addition to finished products, papers showing how students are processing ideas as readers, writers, speakers, and listeners. Drafts showing development through revision are especially helpful as students assess their work. Items that demonstrate how your language users are working with their collections can include

- articles, news briefs, sketches, pictures, or other sources collected and used as the basis for written or oral projects
- reading-response notes that have figured in the planning of a paper and have been incorporated into the final work
- other notes, outlines, journal entries, or evidence of planning for papers written or ready to be drafted
- pieces in which the student is thinking out a problem, considering a topic of interest, or planning something for the future
- freewriting, done either at school or at home
- early drafts of the latest revision of a piece of writing
- notes analyzing the student's latest draft, which may direct subsequent revision
- solicited reactions from classmates or the teacher
- a published piece accompanied by revised manuscripts showing edits
- correspondence from relatives and friends to which students have written a response or to which students need to respond
- tapes of conversations or interviews to which a piece of writing refers or on which it is based

Discourage the inclusion of worksheets, unless they contain good examples of student writing or ideas for future student writing; they tend to obscure the message that language development is a process, a major component of which is the expression of student ideas and opinions.

How to Develop and Use Portfolios *(continued)*

Test results in general do not make good contents for portfolios; however, performance assessments can provide a focused example of both language processing and integration of reading and writing skills. Such performance tests are now frequently structured as realistic tasks that require reading, synthesizing, and reacting to particular texts. These assessments may guide students through planning stages and preliminary drafts and lend themselves directly to self-analysis. These assessments should be included with the final draft.

Keeping Journals

A journal is an excellent addition to a portfolio—and one that teachers report is very successful. Journal keeping develops the habit of recording one's observations, feelings, and ideas. At the same time, it can help tentative writers overcome the reluctance to record thoughts in writing and help them improve fluency.

Success with journals has led teachers to experiment with a variety of types:

PERSONAL JOURNAL This form of journal allows writers to make frequent entries on any topic and for any purpose. This popular and satisfying kind of journal writing develops writing fluency and reveals to students the essential relationship between thinking and writing. (If the journal is kept in the portfolio, you may wish to remind students that you will be viewing the portfolio. Tell students to omit anything they would not be comfortable sharing.)

LITERARY JOURNAL OR READER'S LOG This journal promotes open-ended and freewheeling responses to student reading. Students are usually allowed to structure and organize these journals in any way that satisfies them. The literary journal is a valuable source of notes for oral and written expression; it can also give students ideas for further reading. As with personal journals, literary journals reveal to students that reading, writing, and thinking are interrelated.

TOPICAL JOURNAL This style of journal is dedicated to a particular interest or topic. These journals allow students to express themselves freely about a specific topic—a favorite hobby, pastime, or issue, for example. Topical journals can point students toward project ideas and further reading.

DIALOGUE JOURNAL For this journal format, students select one person—a classmate, friend, family member, or teacher, for example—with whom to have a continuing dialogue. Dialogue journals help develop audience awareness and can promote cooperative learning. If students in your class are

How to Develop and Use Portfolios *(continued)*

You might want to brainstorm a list of things that could be kept in your students' portfolios and then prioritize the items on your list according to which ones you think will be essential for students' development.

keeping dialogue journals with each other, be prepared to help them decide in whose portfolio the journal will go.

What should the criteria be for deciding what will be included?

Teachers often want to ensure that students keep certain kinds of papers in the portfolios, while also promoting a genuine sense of student ownership. Students can be informed that they will be asked to keep certain items as one part of the overall project, including many of the forms provided in this booklet. As they become accustomed to analyzing the papers in their portfolios, students can be encouraged or required to develop criteria and select the contents of their portfolios themselves. Teachers can help students articulate these criteria in informal and formal conferences. Following are criteria teachers or students might consider:

- papers that students think represent their best efforts, or papers that were difficult to complete
- subjects that students enjoyed writing about, or texts they have enjoyed reading; things that they think are interesting or will interest others
- things that relate to reading or writing that students intend to do in the future, including ideas that may be developed into persuasive essays, details to support positions on issues, and reactions to favorite literary texts
- papers that contain ideas or procedures that students wish to remember
- incomplete essays or projects that presented difficulty. Students may plan to ask parents, teachers, or peers to react to their work or to earlier drafts.
- work that students would like particular viewers (the teacher, their parents, their classmates, and so on) to see. This criterion will dictate selections for a show portfolio; it may also determine some of the papers selected for the overall collection.

After building their collections for some time, students should be able to examine them and list their selection criteria in their own words. Doing so should ensure students' sense of ownership.

A final note on selection criteria for student portfolios: While portfolios should certainly contain students' best efforts, too often teachers and students elect to collect only their "best stuff." An overemphasis on possible audiences that might view the collection can make it seem important that the collection be a show portfolio. Preparing show portfolios for particular audiences can require students to assess their work in order to decide what is worth including. That is a worthwhile

How to Develop and Use Portfolios *(continued)*

Start collecting some samples of holders you can show when you introduce portfolio management to your students. Decorate at least one sample, or have a young friend or relative do it. At the same time, be thinking about areas in your classroom where the collections can be kept.

experience, but once the preparation for the show has been completed, student self-assessment ends.

How and where will the portfolio collections be kept?

Part of the fun of keeping portfolios is deciding what the collection holders will look like. In a few classrooms, portfolio holders are standardized, but in most classes, students are allowed to create their own. Many teachers allow students to furnish their own containers or folders, as well as encourage their students to decorate their portfolio holders in unique, colorful, personal, and whimsical ways. Allowing this individuality creates enthusiasm for the project.

Students are likely to bring household cardboard boxes, stationery boxes, folders of various types, paper or plastic shopping bags, computer paper boxes, and plastic and cardboard containers. It would be a good idea to have several different examples to show students when discussing how they will keep their papers. It is also a good idea to have some holders on hand for students who are unable to find anything suitable and to replace unworkable holders.

The resulting storage area probably will not be neatly uniform, but it will not necessarily be unattractive, either. Teachers who want tidier storage areas might find similar boxes to pass out to all students, and then allow them to personalize them.

The amount of space available in a particular classroom will, of course, determine where students keep their collections, but it is vital that the area be accessible and close to students. Students should be able to retrieve and put away their portfolios in less than a minute or two.

Open access to portfolios does create the possibility of students looking at classmates' collections without permission and without warning. Remind students not to include in their portfolio anything they would not want others to see. A teacher's caution could save a student from a wounding embarrassment.

Conferencing with Students

If you are new at conducting portfolio conferences, ask a student who has kept one or more papers to sit down and talk with you. Talk with the student about what he or she thinks is strong about the paper, how it came to be written, and what kind of reading or research the student undertook. See how well you can promote an open-ended conversation related to the topic of the paper and to language use.

Regular informal exchanges between teacher and student about portfolio content are obviously very important, but more formal, anchoring conferences are of equal if not greater importance. Conferences show that teacher and student take the portfolio collection seriously and reinforce the need for ongoing analysis. By blocking out time to conduct at least four formal conferences with each student each year, the teacher demonstrates a commitment to the program and a genuine interest in each student's progress.

Conducting Portfolio Conferences

Conferences should proceed as friendly but clearly directed conversations between student and teacher. The conference should focus on how the use of language serves the student's needs and interests. This focus translates, in the course of the conference, into helping each student reflect on why and how he or she reads and writes.

In conference, teachers will want to discuss with students the quantity of recent writing relative to that of previous time periods; the kinds of writing that the student has done; the student's purposes for writing; how pieces came to be included in the portfolio; and whether the pieces represent experiences and ideas the student has enjoyed and thinks are important. Teachers should let students know that the portfolio documents say something important about the individual student's life. Here are a few examples of questions and statements that might elicit information about a student's interests:

Think about what you could do to ensure a productive portfolio conference that would be helpful and worthwhile to students.

- You seem to know a lot about deep-sea diving.
- Where did you learn all those details?
- Have you looked for books about deep-sea diving?
- What kinds of things could you write about deep-sea diving?

In conference, students, too, should feel free to ask questions:

- Which pieces seem best to the teacher and why?
- Is it always necessary to write for an audience?
- What if I *want* an idea or thought to remain private, though written?
- If I don't know how to spell a certain word, is it OK to just keep writing and look it up later?

Conferences can provide powerful, effective opportunities to teach and to guide language development. Conversations between teachers and students should be as unique as the individual students who join in this exchange.

Conferencing with Students *(continued)*

Ideally, each student will look forward to the conference as a time when student and teacher will pay close attention to the student's accomplishments, feelings about performance, and needs and goals. Such conferences encourage students to accept responsibility for their own development.

The following guidelines will help you make the most of portfolio conferences.

Conference Guidelines

- *Conferences should be conducted without interruption.* Plan creatively: Perhaps a volunteer assistant can manage the rest of the class during meetings. Or, assign to other students learning activities or other work that does not disrupt your exchange with the student. It may be necessary to conduct the conference outside class time.

- *Keep the focus on the student.* Make conference conversations as informal as possible. Ask questions that emphasize the student's interests, attitudes toward writing, and favorite topics. Demonstrate that you care about the student's thoughts and interests. Show that you respect the way a student's individuality is manifested in language use.

- *Let the conversation develop naturally.* Be an active listener. Give full attention to what the student is saying, and respect the course of the exchange. Drop some planned questions so that conferences address individual student interests and needs.

- *Be sincere but not judgmental.* Avoid evaluating or passing judgment on interests or aspects of the student's language use, but try to avoid continually expressing approval. Do not create a situation in which the student responds in order to win favor: The conference will then lose its focus on the individual's language needs and development.

- *Keep the conversation open and positive.* In general, ask questions that promise to open up discussion, not shut it down. Phrase questions and comments so that they invite elaboration and explanation. When necessary, ask questions that direct the focus back to the collection, its ideas and content, the process of writing, and indications of the student's strengths and progress as a language user.

- *Gear the conference toward goal setting.* Identify and come to an agreement about the student's goals and objectives for the next time period.

For many teachers, the time and planning that the conference demands constitute the most difficult aspect of portfolio assessment. Think about how you can use all the resources at your disposal, and don't forget to enlist students' help. Ask them to help you schedule meetings, and request their cooperation so that the system functions smoothly.

Questions will undoubtedly occur to you while reviewing the student's portfolio. It may be useful to have a few notes to remind you of things you would like to ask. Do not, however, approach a conference with a list that dictates the exchange with the student.

Don't hesitate to use the conference as a means of getting to know the student better by learning about his or her interests, pastimes, concerns, and opinions. This can be time well spent, particularly if it demonstrates to the student that the various aspects of his or her life can be very closely connected to the use and development of language arts skills.

Conferencing with Students *(continued)*

- *Limit the attention devoted to usage errors.* If the student needs to focus on mechanical or grammatical problems, tactfully suggest that the student pay particular attention to one or two of these problems when editing and revising. Do not turn the session into a catalogue of encountered language errors. Keep in mind that if each one of four conferences encourages a focus on just one or two types of error, it is possible to eliminate from four to eight high-priority errors during the course of a school year.

- *Keep joint notes with the student on the conference.* To keep a focus on the most important aspects of the conference, you and the student should keep notes, perhaps based on the same observations. For example, the student might write, "I like to use a lot of verbs at the beginning of my sentences, but maybe I use too many." And you might write, "Let's watch to see how often Cody frontshifts sentence elements for emphasis." The student might write, "Look for a novel about the Civil War." You might note, "Find a copy of *The Killer Angels* for Cody." When the two participants make notes on the same sheet, side by side, notes on the same point will roughly correspond. The teacher and the student can even write at the same time if they can position the note sheet comfortably.

Later, you may refer to conference notes as you develop an action plan by completing this book's goal-setting worksheet.

Supplemental Conferences

In addition to scheduled conferences, there are several other types of conferences that teachers can conduct as a part of portfolio assessment:

GOAL CLARIFICATION CONFERENCES If a student appears to be having trouble using the portfolio system, schedule a goal clarification conference. In conference, help the student clarify and articulate objectives so that work on the collection is directed and productive.

Avoid being overly critical. Instead, be supportive and positive about the student's collection; try to lead the student to clear goals. Together, you may articulate these objectives on a goal-setting worksheet.

PUBLICATION STAFF CONFERENCES Students who are publishing pieces may frequently meet as teams or in staff conferences to select from their portfolios. They may also discuss possible revisions of their manuscripts. Teachers may enjoy observing these conferences, but students should direct them as much as possible.

Conferencing with Students *(continued)*

Other class projects and collaborative activities may call for similar student conferences when they involve portfolio collections.

INFORMAL OR ROVING CONFERENCES Teachers sometimes consult with students about their portfolios during impromptu sessions. For example, any time a teacher encounters a student with an important and intriguing question, spots confusion, or discovers frustration, the situation calls for effective questioning and good listening, just as in the regularly scheduled conferences.

Questions and Answers

Teachers who are thinking about instituting a portfolio management system often ask the following questions.

How can I make my students comfortable with portfolios?

Begin by describing what portfolios are and what they are designed to accomplish. One way to help students visualize portfolios is to point out that some professionals keep portfolios:

- Artists usually keep portfolios to show prospective clients or employers what kind of work they can do. In a sense, an artist's studio is one big working portfolio, full of projects in various stages of completion.
- Photographers, architects, clothing designers, interior designers, and a host of other professionals keep portfolios full of samples of their work.
- Models carry portfolios of pictures showing them in a variety of styles and situations.
- Professional writers often keep portfolios of their work.
- People who invest their money in stocks and bonds call a collection of different investments a portfolio.

Teachers can encourage students' interest by inviting to the classroom someone who can exhibit and explain a professional portfolio. Teachers might also show students language arts portfolios created by students in other classes. Some teachers put together their own portfolios and use them as examples for their students.

You might also share the following information with students:

- What kinds of things will go into the portfolios and why? Students can choose what to include in their collections, but teachers can indicate that a few items will be required, including some records. You might show and explain basic forms, such as logs.
- Portfolios will be examined regularly. If the working portfolios will be available to parents or others, be sure to inform students. If you plan for others to see only show portfolios, this might be a good time to introduce this kind of portfolio.
- Show examples of holders and explain where they will be kept. Students can be involved in making decisions about how and where portfolios will be housed.

How often should my students work on their portfolios?

The answer is "regularly and often." Teachers should schedule half-hour sessions weekly; ideally, students should work on their collections daily. The Scheduling Plan on page 133 shows activities that should occur regularly in your program.

Questions and Answers *(continued)*

How can I keep the portfolios from growing too bulky to manage and analyze effectively?

Because portfolios are intended to demonstrate students' products and processes over time, collections should be culled only when necessary. However, when working portfolios become too big, bulky, and clumsy to organize and analyze, encourage students to try one of the following techniques:

- Cull older pieces except for those that stand as the best work examples. Put the removed contents into a separate holder and complete an *About This Portfolio* record. Explain on the record that the work consists of less-favored work, and take it home for parents to examine and/or save. Photocopies of later work that you consider more successful can be included for comparison.

- Close the whole collection, except for writing not yet completed, notes and records, and other idea files. Take the entire collection home with an explanation record, and start a new portfolio.

- Cull from the collection one or more show portfolios for particular audiences, such as parents, other relatives, other teachers, administrators, or supervisors. After the show portfolio has been viewed, return it to the rest of the collection. Start a new portfolio, beginning with the ideas in progress.

Some teachers have their students prepare a larger decorated box to take home at the beginning of the school year. This container may hold banded groups of papers culled during the year. Students then have one repository for their entire portfolio collection, which they can keep indefinitely.

Questions and Answers *(continued)*

SCHEDULING PLAN FOR PORTFOLIO ASSESSMENT

Activity	Frequency	The Student	The Teacher
Keeping logs	As writing and other language experiences are completed; daily if necessary	Makes the entries on the *Writing Record*	Encourages the student to make regular entries and discusses with the student indications of progress, developing interests, etc.
Collecting writing samples, reactions to reading, entries that reflect on oral language	As drafts and reactions to reading become available; can be as often as daily	Selects materials to be included	Can select materials to be included; may require some inclusions
Keeping journal(s)	Ongoing basis; daily to at least once a week	Makes regular entries in one or more journals	Analyzes journal writing discreetly and confidentially
Adding notes, pictures, clippings, and other idea sources	Weekly or more often	Clips and collects ideas and adds them to appropriate places in the portfolio	Reacts to student's idea sources (every month or so); discusses with student how he or she will use them
Explaining, analyzing, evaluating inclusions	Weekly; at least every other week	Uses forms for evaluating and organizing work to analyze and describe individual pieces included	Analyzes inclusions and student analysis of them at least four times a year—before conferences
Completing summary analyses	Monthly and always before conference	Completes a *Summary of Progress* record while comparing it with previously completed summary	Completes selected progress reports at least four times a year—before conferences, relying on student summaries and previously completed records
Conferencing—informal	Ongoing; ideally, at least once a week	Freely asks teacher for advice as often as needed; shares emerging observations with teacher	Makes an effort to observe student working on portfolio at least every two weeks and to discuss one or more specific new inclusions and analyses
Conferencing—formal	At least four times a year	Prepares for conference by completing summaries; discusses portfolio contents and analysis of them with teacher; devises new goals; takes joint notes	Prepares for conference with evaluative analyses; discusses portfolio contents and analysis with student; establishes new goals; takes joint notes
Preparing explanation of portfolio and analysis of it for a particular audience	As occasion for allowing other audiences access arises	Thoughtfully fills out the *About This Portfolio* form	Keeps student advised as to when other audiences might be looking at the student's collection and who the viewer(s) will be
Reacting to a fellow student's paper or portfolio	When it is requested by a partner or other classmate	Conferences with peer	Encourages collaboration whenever possible

Questions and Answers *(continued)*

Should I grade my students' portfolios?

Teachers might be tempted to grade portfolios to encourage student accountability. They may also feel that a grade legitimizes—or at least recognizes—the time and effort that goes into successful portfolio assessment. Finally, many parents, school supervisors, and administrators will expect the teacher to grade the portfolio. These reasons notwithstanding, most portfolio experts advise against grading portfolios. Keep in mind that the collection will contain papers that have been graded. A grade for the collection as a whole, however, risks undermining the goals of portfolio management. Grading portfolios may encourage students to include only their "best" work, and that practice may convey the message that student self-assessment is not taken seriously.

Who, besides the student and me, should see the portfolio?

This question raises some of the same concerns as the issue of grading portfolios. Teachers may feel some responsibility to let parents, a supervisor, the principal, and fellow faculty members know how the program, the class, or individuals are progressing. Balance the benefits of showing portfolios to outside audiences against the possible adverse effects—the risk of inhibiting students, diminishing their sense of ownership, or invading their privacy. Above all, keep in mind the primary aims of portfolio assessment.

Following are some suggestions for showing portfolios, with respect to audience.

PARENTS OR GUARDIANS Family members will almost certainly view the portfolio in one form or another. If parents or other responsible adults are to view collections on more formal occasions, such as back-to-school nights or during unscheduled visits to the classroom, students should be assisted in creating show portfolios. If, on the other hand, portfolios are to be shown without the owners' knowledge or opportunity for review, the teacher must tell students this at the beginning of the year. Warning students of these unscheduled viewings may qualify their sense of ownership; it can also intensify their audience awareness.

SCHOOL SUPERVISORS AND PRINCIPALS Students' portfolios can demonstrate to fellow educators how youngsters develop as language users, thinkers, and people; they can also show the kind of learning that is taking place in the classroom. When showing working portfolios, select at random from those kept in the class, and mask the owners' identities. Choosing between working or show collections (assuming the state or

---

Another way to involve parents in portfolio management is to let students plan a workshop on portfolio management geared for parents and others who are interested. Or, as suggested earlier, have students cull their collections periodically and take the materials home for their parents to see.

Again, if portfolios will be shown to other educators, students should be made aware of this before they start to build their collections.

Questions and Answers *(continued)*

school system does not mandate them) may depend partly on whether the audience will be able to appreciate the progress and process displayed by working collections.

CLASSMATES Students may review their peers' portfolios as part of the program's assessment. Even if a particular program does not include a formal peer-review stage, remind students that peers may see their collections—either in the process of collaborative work or peer review, or because a student does not respect the privacy of others.

NEXT YEAR'S TEACHERS At the end of the school year, teachers can help students create show portfolios for their next teacher or teachers. The show portfolio should demonstrate the student's growth during the year, the potential of his or her best efforts, and the most recent goals established by the teacher and the student.

Encourage students to include finished projects as well as earlier drafts. Discuss what kinds of logs should be included, or have students prepare a brief report showing how goals have been met. A fresh table of contents would be useful, as would an explanation of the show collection's purpose. Teachers may want to let students take copies of some papers home.

How can I protect against the possible negative effects of allowing a wide variety of persons to see students' portfolios?

When portfolios are used for special reporting, the teacher needs to offset any possible adverse effects by keeping the primary aims for portfolio assessment in mind.

- The overall goal of the program is to develop students as language users. That goal should be the focus of joint student/teacher evaluation of the student's progress.
- Collections must be readily available to students so that they may develop a habit of self-assessment.
- Emphasis should be on examining the process by looking at the product and the way it is produced. Each portfolio should contain a working collection of notes, drafts, and records evaluating contents.
- Assessed activities should integrate reading, writing, speaking, and listening.
- The portfolio should be controlled and owned by the student.
- The collections should include reactions to and applications of a variety of text and writing types—with a variety of purposes involving different audiences.

Portfolio Table of Contents

Decide on the major categories for work in your portfolio. Then, in the sections below, list the categories you have chosen. The works themselves may be papers, speech notecards, videotapes, multimedia products, or any work you and your teacher agree should be included. In choosing categories, consider organizing work by topic, by genre (essays, poems, stories, and so on), by chronology (work completed by month, for example), by level of difficulty (work that was less difficult, somewhat difficult, and more difficult), or by another category.

Grade: ________________   **School year:** ________________________

▶ WORK IN EACH SECTION	▶ WHY I PUT THIS WORK IN THIS SECTION
Section 1:	
title:	
title:	
title:	
title:	
Section 2:	
title:	
title:	
title:	
title:	
Section 3:	
title:	
title:	
title:	
title:	

About This Portfolio

Use this form whenever you are preparing your portfolio for review by your teacher or another reader.

Grade: _______________ **School year:** _______________ **When I began this portfolio:** _______________

▶ **How it is organized:**

▶ **What I think it shows about my progress ...**

as a reader:

as a writer:

as a listener:

as a speaker:

GO ON ➡

About This Portfolio *(continued)*

▶ **Examples of My Best Work**

The best things I have read are—	Why I like them—
The best things I have written are—	Why I like them—
Other things in my portfolio that I hope you notice are— 1. 2. 3.	What they show—

Examples of My Best Work

TO PARENT OR GUARDIAN

Home Review: What the Portfolio Shows

In the left-hand column of the chart below, I have noted what I believe this portfolio shows about your student's development in areas such as reading, writing, speaking, and listening. The right-hand column notes where you can look for evidence of that development.

A prime objective in keeping portfolios is to help students develop a habit of analyzing and evaluating their work. This portfolio includes work that the student has collected over a period of time. Your student has decided what to include but has been encouraged to include different types of writing, responses to reading, and evidence of other uses of language. Many of the writings included are accompanied by earlier drafts and plans that show how the work has evolved from a raw idea to a finished piece of writing. Drafts are included to reinforce the idea that using language entails a process of revision and refinement.

▶ I believe that this portfolio shows—	▶ To see evidence of this, please notice—

Teacher's signature____

TO PARENT OR GUARDIAN

Home Response to the Portfolio

▶ Please answer any questions that seem important to you. Use the reverse side for any additional comments or questions.

Parent or Guardian _________________________________ Date _________________

What did you learn from the portfolio about your child's reading?

____

____

What did you learn from the portfolio about your child's writing?

____

____

Were you surprised by anything in the portfolio? Why?

____

____

What do you think is the best thing in the portfolio? What do you like about it?

____

____

Do you have questions about anything in the portfolio? What would you like to know more about?

____

____

What does the portfolio tell you about your child's progress as a writer, reader, and thinker?

____

____

Do you think keeping a portfolio has had an effect on your child as a reader or writer—or in another way? If so, what?

____

____

Is there anything missing from the portfolio that you would have liked or had expected to see? If so, what?

____

____

　

SELF-EVALUATION

Writing Record

> **Ratings:** ✓✓✓✓ One of my best!   ✓✓ OK, but not my best
>   ✓✓✓ Better if I revise it   ✓ I don't like this one.

▶ Month/Day	▶ Title and type of writing	▶ Notes about this piece of writing	▶ Rating

Spelling Log

▶ Word	▶ My misspelling	▶ How to remember correct spelling

Goal-Setting for Writing, Listening, and Speaking

GOAL	STEPS TO REACH GOAL	REVIEW OF PROGRESS
Writing Goals		

Goal-Setting for Writing, Listening, and Speaking *(continued)*

▶ GOAL	▶ STEPS TO REACH GOAL	▶ REVIEW OF PROGRESS
Listening Goals		
Speaking Goals		

Summary of Progress: Writing, Listening, and Speaking

Complete this form before sitting down with your teacher or a classmate to assess your overall progress, set goals, or discuss specific pieces of your work.

Grade : _______________   **School year:** _______________   **Date of summary:** _______________

▶ **What work have I done so far this year?**

Writing:

Listening:

Speaking:

▶ **What project do I plan to work on next?**

Writing:

Listening:

Speaking:

▶ **What do I think of my progress?**

What about my work has improved?

What needs to be better?

▶ **Which examples of work are my favorites and why?**

Summary of Progress: Writing, Listening, and Speaking *(continued)*

▶ **Which pieces of work need more revision, and what revision is needed?**

▶ **How has listening or speaking helped me in preparing for papers or other projects this year?**

▶ **What a classmate or the teacher thinks about my progress**

In writing—

In listening—

In speaking—

SELF-EVALUATION

Writing Self-Inventory

Questions and answers about my writing	More about my answers
How often do I write?	What types of writing do I do?
Where, besides school, do I write?	What kind of writing do I do there?
Do I like to write?	Why or why not?
Of the things I have written, I like these best:	Why do I like them best?
What topics do I like to write about?	Why do I like to write about these topics?
Is anything about writing difficult for me? What?	Why do I think it is difficult?
Does reading help me to be a better writer or vice versa?	Why do I think this?
How important is learning to write well?	Why do I think this?

Writing Process Self-Evaluation

Choose one paper from your portfolio, preferably one for which you have your prewriting notes and all your drafts. Use the chart below to analyze your writing process. Circle the numbers that most clearly indicate how well you meet the stated criteria in your writing process. The lowest possible total score is 5, the highest, 20.

1 = Does not meet these criteria

2 = Attempts to meet these criteria but needs to improve

3 = Meets these criteria fairly successfully

4 = Clearly meets these criteria

Title of paper ____

STAGE IN WRITING PROCESS	CRITERIA FOR EVALUATION	RATING
Prewriting	■ Use prewriting techniques to find and limit subject and to gather details about subject ■ Organize details in a reasonable way	1 2 3 4
Writing	■ Get most of ideas down on paper in a rough draft	1 2 3 4
Revising	■ Complete peer- or self-evaluation ■ Find ways to improve content, organization, and style of rough draft ■ Revise by adding, cutting, replacing, and moving material	1 2 3 4
Proofreading	■ Correct errors in spelling, grammar, usage, punctuation, capitalization, and manuscript form	1 2 3 4
Publishing and Reflecting	■ Produce a clean final copy in proper form ■ Share the piece of writing with others ■ Reflect on the writing process and on the paper's strengths and weaknesses	1 2 3 4

Additional Comments:

Proofreading Strategies

Proofread your paper using one of the following steps. Put a check by the step you used.

_____   **1.** Read the paper backward word by word.

_____   **2.** Make a large card with a one- or two-inch-sized strip cut into it and read every word in the paper, one at a time, through the hole.

_____   **3.** Read the first sentence in your paper carefully. Put your left index finger on the punctuation mark that signals the end of that sentence. Now, put your right index finger on the punctuation mark that ends the second sentence. Carefully read the material between your fingers; then, move your left index finger to the end of the second sentence and your right to the end of the third sentence, and read carefully. Keep moving your fingers until you have carefully examined each sentence in the paper.

List the mistakes you discovered when proofreading.

____

____

____

____

____

____

____

____

____

____

____

Proofreading Checklist

Read through the paper and then mark the following statements either **T** for true or **F** for false. If you are reviewing a classmate's paper, return the paper and checklist to the writer. After the writer has done his or her best to correct the paper, offer to assist if your help is needed.

Writer's name _________________________________ **Title of paper** _________________________________

_____ **1.** The paper is neat.

_____ **2.** Each sentence begins with a capital letter.

_____ **3.** Each sentence ends with a period, question mark, or exclamation mark.

_____ **4.** Each sentence is complete. Each has a subject and a predicate and expresses a complete thought.

_____ **5.** The paper contains no run-on sentences.

_____ **6.** A singular verb is used with each singular subject and a plural verb with each plural subject.

_____ **7.** Nominative case pronouns such as *I* and *we* are used for subjects; objective case pronouns such as *me* and *us* are used for objects.

_____ **8.** Singular pronouns refer to singular nouns, and plural pronouns refer to plural nouns.

_____ **9.** The paper contains no indefinite pronoun references.

_____ **10.** Each word is spelled correctly.

_____ **11.** Frequently confused words, such as *lie/lay*, *sit/set*, *rise/raise*, *all ready/already*, and *fewer/less*, are used correctly.

_____ **12.** The paper contains no double negatives.

_____ **13.** All proper nouns and proper adjectives are capitalized.

_____ **14.** Word endings such as *–s*, *–ing*, and *–ed* are included where they should be.

_____ **15.** No words have been accidentally left out or accidentally written twice.

_____ **16.** Each paragraph is indented.

_____ **17.** Apostrophes are used correctly with contractions and possessive nouns.

_____ **18.** Commas or pairs of commas are used correctly.

_____ **19.** Dialogue is punctuated and capitalized correctly.

_____ **20.** Any correction that could not be rewritten or retyped is crossed out with a single line.

Record of Proofreading Corrections

Keeping a record of the kinds of mistakes you make can be helpful. For the next few writing assignments, list the errors you, your teacher, or your peers find in your work. If you faithfully use this kind of record, you'll find it easier to avoid troublesome errors.

Writer's name ______________________________ **Title of paper** ______________________

Write sentences that contain errors in grammar or usage here.   **Write corrections here.**

Write sentences that contain errors in mechanics here.   **Write corrections here.**

Write misspelled words and corrections here.

Multiple-Assignment Proofreading Record

DIRECTIONS: When your teacher returns a corrected writing assignment, write the title or topic on the appropriate vertical line at right. Under the title or topic, record the number of errors you made in each area. Use this sheet when you proofread your next assignment, taking care to check those areas in which you make frequent mistakes.

TITLE OR TOPIC OF ASSIGNMENT

Type of Error

Sentence Fragments

Run-on Sentences

Incorrect Subject-Verb Agreement

Incorrect Pronoun Agreement

Incorrect Pronoun Form

Use of Double Negative

Incorrect Comparison of Adjectives or Adverbs

Confusing Verbs

Incorrect Irregular Verb Forms

Incorrect Noun Plurals or Possessives

Incorrect Capitalization

Misspellings

Incorrect or Missing End Punctuation

Incorrect Use of Apostrophes

Confusing Words

Incorrect Use of Quotation Marks or Italics

Incorrect Use of Comma or Paired Commas

Listening Self-Inventory

Questions and answers about my listening	More about my answers
What kinds of music do I like to listen to?	Why do I like them?
What TV shows and movies are my favorites?	What do I like about them?
How well do I listen in school?	How much do I learn by listening?
Do I listen carefully to what my friends say?	What do I learn from them?
When is it difficult for me to listen?	What makes it difficult?
How do I use the praise and suggestions of others to improve my skills?	How do I feel about getting praise or suggestions for improvement?

Speaking Self-Inventory

▶ Questions and answers about my speaking	▶ More about my answers
How effective are my speaking skills when I am talking to friends?	What do I like to discuss with them?
How effective are my speaking skills when I am talking to adults?	When do I feel comfortable talking with them?
How effective are my speaking skills when I am reciting or speaking to the class?	When do I feel comfortable speaking to the class?
What is the most difficult thing about speaking?	Why is it difficult?
What techniques have I learned to improve my speaking skills?	How do I use these techniques with friends or in class?

Skills Profile

Student's Name _______________________ Grade _______________

Teacher's Name _______________________ Date _______________

For each skill, write the date the observation is made and any comments that explain the student's development toward skills mastery.

SKILL	NOT OBSERVED	EMERGING	PROFICIENT
Writing			
Writing Modes			
Write a reflective essay.			
Write an essay analyzing problems and solutions.			
Write an essay persuading with cause and effect.			
Write an extended definition.			
Write an editorial examining a controversial issue.			

GO ON

SKILL	NOT OBSERVED	EMERGING	PROFICIENT
Write an essay analyzing literature.			
Write a research paper.			
Writing Process			
Prewriting			
• Choose a topic.			
• Identify purpose and audience.			
• Generate ideas and gather information about the topic.			
• Begin to organize the information.			
• Draft a thesis statement, or a sentence that expresses the main point.			

GO ON

Skills Profile *(continued)*

SKILL	NOT OBSERVED	EMERGING	PROFICIENT
Writing a Draft			
• State the main points and include relevant support and elaboration.			
• Follow a plan of organization.			
Revising			
• Revise for content and style.			
Publishing			
• Proofread for grammar, usage, and mechanics.			
• Publish the work, or share the finished writing with readers.			
• Reflect on the writing experience.			

GO ON

SKILL	NOT OBSERVED	EMERGING	PROFICIENT
Listening and Speaking			
Present and evaluate a speech.			
Give a persuasive speech.			
Present a literary analysis.			
Present research.			
Analyze media.			
Use media.